The Cockroach that *Saved* My Marriage

Sonal Lobo

INDIA • SINGAPORE • MALAYSIA

ISBN 979-8-89133-935-4

Contents

Acknowledgement

I would like to begin by expressing my heartfelt gratitude to Almighty God for showering His blessings upon me and bestowing upon me the gift of writing. I am truly thankful for the opportunities He has provided me to showcase my talents.

I hold in high regard my parents, Godwin Lobo and Precilla Lobo, for their unwavering support and encouragement. They have been with me every step of the way, from the inception to the completion of my writing journey.

A special thanks goes to my dear friend, Vidhya Holla, who has been a constant source of support. Her assistance in editing my writings and helping me present them in the best possible manner has been invaluable.

I am deeply indebted to my better half, Santhosh Christopher D'Almeida, whose encouragement has been the driving force behind all my dreams and endeavours. His unwavering support has meant the world to me.

A heartfelt shout-out to the Notion Press team, whose unwavering support and guidance have been instrumental in turning my publishing dream into a reality. I am grateful for their wonderful collaboration and assistance throughout this journey.

1. Introduction

Have you ever imagined if our lives were like the exciting stories in movies? Full of love, mystery, romance, and even scary moments? Well, someone shared this idea with me once. They wished our days were more thrilling and less ordinary—a break from the usual routine of home, work, and unexciting weekends.

For a short time, I agreed with this thought. I thought life could be more like a movie. But everything changed when I got married. Marriage became a fascinating journey that completely changed how I saw things. Meeting different people and facing various situations made me laugh, cry, and learn important lessons. This book is about the things that happened after I got married, the lessons I learned, and the truths I discovered.

Life is like an adventure, a mix of happiness and challenges, shaped by how we see things. A rainy day might be annoying if you're stuck in traffic, but it's a blessing for a farmer's thirsty crops. Just like a bone in your food might bother you, it could be a treat for a hungry dog. With these thoughts, I want to share seemingly small moments from my journey that had a big impact on me. These stories helped me become a better person.

Come with me on this journey down memory lane. You'll find funny and touching stories that will make you laugh and think. Life is full of surprises, and I can't wait to share the lessons I've learned along the way.

2. My Matchmaking Misadventure: When My Plan Backfired

In a typical Indian family, after completing studies and starting work, the topic of marriage comes into play. As the only daughter, I never anticipated this, as my dad had never mentioned marriage before. Everything seemed calm until one day, out of the blue, my dad dropped a bombshell: I needed to get married within a year.

Caught off guard, I was at a loss for words. Since I had never said no to my dad, I quietly agreed. The whirlwind began—photo shoots, exchanging photos and biodata—but despite the frenzy, no suitable match seemed to emerge.

I didn't have high expectations. My criteria were basic but a bit unusual: I wanted a simple, humble, God-fearing guy, and importantly, not conventionally handsome. I had a different perspective and wasn't seeking the typical tall, dark, and handsome type.

And so began the great Indian matchmaking saga. Profiles flowed in, and my details were shared with numerous potential matches. However, nothing seemed to align with my preferences. Not being in the mood for marriage, I wasn't bothered.

Then, a close relative introduced me to what they believed was the most eligible guy. I was asked to share my profile and photo and check him out on social media. My first impression was a firm "no!" He was the opposite of what I was looking for—remarkably handsome and far from simple. I declined, and to my surprise, I later learned that he had also rejected me for not meeting his criteria. This brought relief to me and him, but disappointment to others involved.

However, the story didn't end there. Despite my initial rejection, my relatives persisted, and, after much coaxing, I reluctantly agreed to meet this "not my type" guy. I made it clear to my parents that I was going along just for the sake of it and would put on an act if they pushed for a positive response.

Our meeting was set for a Sunday, and I counted down the days with a sense of burden. I didn't want this proposal to succeed. Deep down, I was sure he would reject me as well, given that his agreement to meet was likely influenced by his parents.

I prepared my strategy. I spoke to friends and colleagues and even conducted extensive online research on "qualities men dislike in women." After much exploration, I discovered that many men dislike women who ask too many questions and seem overly inquisitive.

The meeting day finally arrived. Exhausted from an exam, I arrived at the relative's house without putting much effort into my appearance. I deliberately looked my worst. When we were given a chance to talk privately on the terrace, I wasted no time. I bombarded him with questions about his life, habits, and past relationships. I barely let him speak, satisfied that my plan was working.

After our conversation, he and his parents bid farewell, and I was convinced it was the end of the story. I was confident he wouldn't look back. However, to my shock and dismay, I received a call later informing me that he had shown interest in marrying me. I was frustrated; my plan had backfired.

With a heavy heart, I eventually said yes to this man. And here comes the twist: We got married and now live happily together.

Looking back, it's amusing. I had tried everything to push him away, yet he turned out to be the one for me. When I asked him why he had agreed to marry me despite initially rejecting me, he revealed that he had always wanted a talkative partner, not a quiet one.

I chuckled at the irony. My plan wasn't flawed; it was just misapplied to the wrong person. Perhaps if I had chosen to remain quiet, he might have said no. Or maybe not?

This incident reminds me that whatever happens, it's often for the best. We may complain, argue, and cry, but in the end, things usually work out. I still talk a lot, and I always will. Deep down, I offer a silent thank you; speaking up that day led me to the most precious gift of my life.

3. Sharing: A Lesson in Caring

All of us have special things in our lives. Some people cherish their books, while others love their toys or accessories. There are things we want to keep forever and never let go of.

But there's a difference between keeping something as a memory and holding onto things because we don't want to share them. In my family, I've seen some people who refuse to part with their toys, even if they're over 20 years old. Some can't let go of clothes that don't fit anymore, and others keep tiny shoes. The list goes on.

My mom used to complain that I gave things away too easily, without even thinking if I still needed them. Even though I was the only child and didn't need to share, an incident from my childhood changed me. I now find joy in giving things away.

Most girls love their clothes. When I was younger, I adored my clothes too. Giving them away felt like the worst punishment. I'd keep them safe and never share them with anyone. My collection of clothes made me happy.

I remember when I was about 8 years old, I had a beautiful white skirt with pink flowers. It was my favorite. I took great care of it. I received compliments, and some people even wanted a similar skirt. I felt proud of owning such a unique dress. I wore it for over 2 years, but as I grew taller, it became too short. Even though I couldn't wear it anymore, I kept it safely on my shelf.

During Christmas, we have a lovely tradition of giving away old clothes to the church for the less fortunate. One Christmas, my mom insisted that I give away my favorite skirt. I didn't want to. I protested and cried, but my mom was determined. She said it would be given away.

I resisted. I gave reasons why I should keep it, like it being my favorite and how others might not take care of it like I did. But my mom didn't give in. Maybe she wanted me to learn the value of sharing. Reluctantly, I gave in and handed over the skirt, tears in my eyes. It made me sad for a while, but I eventually accepted that the skirt was no longer mine.

About 6 months later, I was attending Sunday mass when my mom pointed out a girl near the church gate. She was wearing my white skirt. I felt a mix of surprise and happiness. I didn't know if I was happy to see my dress or happy that someone was wearing it. Seeing that little girl proudly show off my dress made me feel strangely joyful. The dress still looked beautiful, and it suited her perfectly.

That day, I understood the happiness of giving. I realized I wouldn't have treasured that dress as much as that girl did. For her, it might have been one of her few dresses. The happiness I felt seeing her wear my dress was greater than when I wore it myself. I learned not only to give but to give with a happy heart.

Sometimes we hesitate to share our things with those who have less, thinking they won't appreciate it. But they understand its value even more, as it might be all they have. Trust me, the joy of seeing them treasure something you once loved is immeasurable.

Don't miss a chance to give to others, because when we share, we truly show that we care.

4. With Love: For Those Who Deserve Our Love

Someone I know once said, “You’re really good at writing. Everyone in my family enjoys reading what you write. But why do you always write about your parents?” She went on to suggest that I don’t need to showcase my love for them through writing. She believed it should remain in my heart, and I should focus on addressing important societal issues instead.

I chose not to respond directly, and this article can be seen as my subtle answer to her thought-provoking question.

People often say that our talents are gifts from a higher power, and how we use them becomes our way of giving back. What better use of these talents than to express our deep affection and respect for our parents?

Personally, I enjoy writing about my parents because of the valuable upbringing, guidance, and unwavering support they’ve given me.

Their love and sacrifice were evident from the very beginning. My grandmother used to tell me how my mom faced immense challenges during her pregnancy. Despite poverty and pain, my parents chose to nurture me in the womb, even when some doctors advised otherwise.

I remember times when my parents would eat simple meals like radishes and beets every day, setting aside a bit of meat for me due to limited resources.

They toiled tirelessly at their jobs, working shifts to ensure I could attend a top-notch school and receive the best education.

They always encouraged my talents without imposing their own desires on me. They turned our small house into a warm and loving home through their dedication.

This tribute isn't only for my parents; it's for all parents who silently shoulder every burden, handle every insecurity, wipe away every tear, and put their children's happiness above all else. They seek no reward except love and time.

I remember writing my first piece when I was just 10. It got published in a newspaper after being submitted to school. The joy and pride my parents showed that day remain unforgettable. Even now, nearly two decades later, my parents continue to celebrate even the simplest of my articles. Their constant support has lifted me during times of doubt when I considered giving up writing.

My first piece about my parents was during college. The tears of pride and happiness in my dad's eyes stayed with me. That's when I realized that I would always write about them in every possible way. It was my way of expressing gratitude for all they've done.

Many of us possess numerous talents, but how often do we use them to bring joy to our parents? While it's great to showcase our abilities to the world, have we taken a moment to share them with our parents?

While we're young, we're often with our parents, but as we grow and start our own families, it's vital to spend precious moments with them and express gratitude.

True, parents don't demand anything in return. Rarely have I heard my parents discuss their hardships or ask for something in exchange. But shouldn't we show gratitude for all they've done?

I've attended funerals where children weep on stage, expressing gratitude for their deceased parents. I've wondered why they couldn't show the same appreciation when their parents were alive, letting them know how much they meant.

We expect acknowledgment at work, certificates for achievements, "I love you" messages from our partners, and birthday wishes from relatives. Why is it so challenging to say a simple "THANK YOU" to our parents?

Expressing gratitude doesn't have to be just words; it can be gestures. A surprise dinner, a vacation, new clothes, accompanying them to appointments, or a daily phone call—there are numerous ways to show appreciation and love.

I've chosen writing as my way of thanking my parents for the wonderful life they've given me. I encourage each of you to take a small step today to let your parents know that you recognize their efforts and love them for all they've done, are doing, and will do.

5. Surprised by an Unexpected Surprise

Every girl dreams of a prince on a white horse, sweeping her away to a fairytale land. Well, my dream guy drove a Maruti K10 and totally surprised me.

Us ladies, we're somehow really into special days—birthdays, Valentine's Day, anniversaries. We expect something extraordinary. Sadly, my first wedding anniversary wasn't a celebration due to my sister-in-law's wedding. Her big day was just two days after ours, so any plans for a second honeymoon went out the window. But my husband made up for it with a meaningful dinner where we opened up, patched things up, and pledged to make our love even stronger.

The second year of marriage went smoothly. We stayed true to our promise and grew closer. After the letdown of the first anniversary, I decided our second should be unforgettable. But then, relatives planned to visit for ten days, just around our anniversary. It was a bit of a downer, as my private celebration was getting crowded, but I was happy to be around our loving cousins. My husband promised a candlelight dinner once everyone left.

I've got to say, my man isn't much for romance. Like most guys, he's not big on sweeping gestures. On our first Valentine's Day before marriage, I was super excited and expected loads of flowers and chocolates. Instead, my dream man showed up with just a chocolate bar and took me out for dinner. When I asked about the roses, he gave me money and said I could buy as many as I wanted. That's when I realized he's not the overly romantic type.

A few days after the relatives left, we decided on a nice, quiet restaurant. Like always, I found the best spot after lots of research and reading reviews. I made the bookings and told my husband where and when. In the evening, we got ready and drove to the restaurant. I was excited, and why not? It was an artistically designed place with a cave theme—one of the fanciest spots around.

Inside, a stylishly dressed lady at the reception handed me a huge bouquet of beautiful roses. She wished us a happy second wedding anniversary. I was taken aback and not sure how to react.

But that wasn't the end of the surprise. She led us to a table with a big cake, and the restaurant staff gathered around, singing for us before we cut the cake. We took pictures and enjoyed the cake before settling down to order. I was happy, and more than surprised, I was touched by my husband's gesture. I'd wrongly believed he wasn't romantic, but he'd put in so much effort—picking the flowers and cake, planning this whole thing for me. Just as I was about to thank him, he thanked me.

I was puzzled—why was he thanking me? I was supposed to thank him for planning the surprise. It turns out we both thought the other had planned it. But after thinking it through, we realized neither of us had done it, and no one else could have either.

We were left baffled, wondering who had set this up. It was our first time at that restaurant, and we hadn't shared any details with them. Our friends and family didn't know about our plans either. While we puzzled over this, my eyes landed on the half-eaten cake, and I could read half of the word "anniversary" and some other words ending with

"K." That's when we understood—another couple had planned this, and the restaurant mixed us up.

Feeling a bit embarrassed, we called the receptionist and explained that we were celebrating our second anniversary but hadn't asked for cake and flowers. She apologized, explaining that another couple was celebrating their anniversary. We returned the flowers, but she insisted on bringing a new bouquet. As for the cake, the restaurant manager wouldn't let us pay for it, considering it a small gift from them.

After the confusion settled, we enjoyed our meal and laughed heartily. We talked about how we both thought the other had organized it and how happy we had been. It was a delightful mix-up, creating a memory to cherish.

Even now, on special occasions, we remember cutting someone else's cake and posing with flowers meant for someone else. Whenever we visit a restaurant, we make it clear that we haven't made any plans.

I'm still grateful for that day. It was only a few minutes, but it was beautiful and unforgettable. Sometimes, God turns an ordinary moment into something extraordinary. Even if we had celebrated our anniversary differently, I doubt the memory would be as cherished as this one. Whenever we think back to that day, my husband bursts into laughter, and I offer thanks for the day, wishing that other couple a beautiful, enduring marriage.

6. Suffering in Silence

Reading newspapers or watching the news nowadays is truly disheartening. All we encounter is negative news that leaves a bitter taste and brings sadness to anyone who reads it. Recently, on a social networking platform, I came across an article about a tragic incident where a 12-year-old girl was abused and killed by her own relatives. I also read that many people were protesting and urging the legal system to take swift action. It's heartening to see the public stepping up to support the grieving parents, but it's distressing that yet another innocent girl fell victim to her family's conflicts.

Contemplating this issue, I began to wonder about the various ways women are targeted and mistreated. While major problems are highlighted, what about the smaller, hidden issues? The pain often goes unnoticed. I want to shed light on some seemingly trivial matters that most women endure silently.

From a young age, girls are expected to conform to societal norms and biases. I recall an incident where a friend shared her passion for martial arts over coffee. Despite her athleticism and aspirations to master karate, her parents forbade her from pursuing it, deeming it a pursuit meant for boys. Instead, she was made to take dance classes, even though she had no interest in them. This kind of situation is all too common, where parents impose their dreams on their children. While it's fine if the children are content, it's unfair to force them into activities they dislike. It's time to eliminate gender distinctions and openly encourage girls to pursue their interests. It's disheartening that in a rapidly advancing world, some parents still believe educating girls is less important than marrying them off. Countless intelligent and ambitious girls suffer in silence because they lack the means to express their desires for learning and self-fulfillment.

The next significant step in a girl's life is marriage, a complex process difficult to capture in words. I won't share others' experiences, but I'll share my own. Having a heavier build, I was frequently body-shamed and urged to lose weight, not for my health but to improve my marriage prospects. I recall an insulting comment from a relative during a family gathering. She expressed doubts about finding an educated groom for me due to my weight, criticizing my clothing choices, and suggesting that marrying an older man would be more suitable. These comments hurt, yet they highlighted the constant pressure for women to conform. If a man has flaws, it's acceptable, but if a woman does, she's considered choosy or arrogant. Moreover, if a girl dresses modernly, she's judged and labeled with questionable morals. The journey toward marriage often involves enduring insults and pain in silence.

After marriage, a woman is expected to adhere to her in-laws' standards in dress and behavior. I struggle to comprehend why a woman must compromise her aspirations in the name of adjustment. A colleague shared an incident involving a marriage proposal. She was asked not to work for a year after marriage to avoid upsetting the jobless sister of the groom. This unequal treatment astounded me, and I was relieved when she rejected the proposal. Why should a woman surrender her dreams because of marriage? Friends who were talented singers, dancers, artists, and painters have abandoned their passions due to in-law and spousal expectations. Why aren't women encouraged? It's unjust to strip women of their identity and dreams.

While a woman is expected to adapt to her new family and maintain family unity, what if the new family isn't supportive? Society forgets that efforts should come from both sides. Married women who choose to live separately from their in-laws are often blamed for separating husbands from parents, ignoring the woman's perspective. Sometimes, women endure serious abuse and are denied basic freedoms. When they seek justice, they're accused of having an attitude and causing family discord. In households where both daughters and daughters-in-law coexist, harm befalling the daughter-in-law is brushed aside, while the same hardships for one's own daughter are deemed unfortunate. This unjust favoritism subjects' countless women to silent suffering.

Raping and abusing women is an atrocious crime, but let's not forget that crushing a woman's dreams and passions is also not acceptable. When a woman defies this and pursues her dreams, she faces judgment. I recall when I decided to publish my poetry book; only my husband and parents supported me. Others ridiculed and dismissed my efforts. Nonetheless, I persevered and published my first poetry book, receiving genuine compliments and appreciation despite the judgment. Marriage shouldn't erase a woman's connection to her parents. Just as it's a man's responsibility to care for his parents, it's equally a woman's responsibility to care for hers.

Protests and marches demanding justice for women are important, but we must also fight for justice within our homes. Whether it's your wife, sister, mother, daughter-in-law, or anyone else, respect begins at home. Respecting a woman entails more than providing basic needs; it means granting her the freedom and space to voice her thoughts. Treating women with dignity and equality is pivotal to reducing crimes against them. When you offer support, a woman will wholeheartedly contribute to the family, a fact often forgotten. Women possess immense untapped talent; let's not disregard their needs and desires.

Let's create platforms that empower them to break free from constraints and become their best selves.

Ultimately, remember this: a happy woman translates to a happy family. Let's intensify our efforts to combat injustice against women and end the silent suffering that persists.

7. Learning the Art of Prayer from My Grandmother

Every relationship necessitates time and effort; it demands both quality time and abundant patience.

In our day-to-day lives, no matter how busy we become, we tend to create moments for our loved ones. When they're near, we share meals, tuck them in, or simply sit together watching television. Even when apart, we reach out through calls, texts, or inquiries about their well-being. Upon reflection, we realize that neglecting these connections can lead to resentment and frustration. Although there are days when I prefer solitude and stay hidden, the pressure not to offend drives me to gather courage and share moments.

Like all relationships, our connection with God is of equal importance. For most, God is all-powerful, caring, and the provider of our desires. Prayer serves as our means of communicating with Him and spending time in His presence.

But what is prayer exactly? I've heard numerous sermons and teachings stating that prayer is communication with God. It's not merely us making requests; it's about seeking God and waiting for Him to respond. My prayer journey has been somewhat erratic. On some days, I wait in silence, while on others, I shed tears, feeling distant from Him. Often, I lose enthusiasm and interest, either because I fail to perceive His message or struggle to comprehend how He wishes to converse with me. And then there are days when I simply don't make the effort to pray due to a busy schedule, work commitments, or, quite frankly, laziness.

Recently, during a challenging phase of my prayer life due to my seemingly busy schedule, I recalled a childhood memory. Many of my summer vacations were spent in Mangalore, where my grandmother, Rosy Lobo, showered me with affection. Although she has passed away and is now in her heavenly abode, I often reminisce about her and the moments we shared.

She was a capable and energetic woman of short stature (many do say I resemble her), who single-handedly raised six sons and three daughters while my grandpa served in the navy, often away at sea. Even after her children got married and her daughters-in-law took over household responsibilities, she never idled; she worked tirelessly, always infused with love.

One night during a summer vacation when I was around 6 or 7 years old, I noticed a faint flicker of light in the dining area late at night. Intrigued, I approached cautiously and found my grandma engrossed in reading the Bible. I stood by the door, observing her immersed in her reading, surrounded by a few prayer books. Though I didn't fully grasp the depth of her devotion, I retired to sleep. The following morning, without posing any questions, I began to closely observe her, a ritual that persisted for days and years.

Several years later, at around 15 years of age, I finally mustered the courage to ask her about her nightly prayer routine. I sat beside her one fine day and inquired why she devotedly prayed late into the night every day. I had noticed her praying sometimes at midnight or even later, especially during family gatherings or functions. She never missed a day, whether it was raining, cold, or scorching hot. I was aware that, given her age, she needed good sleep after a tiring day of work. With a gentle tone, I suggested that it was okay to skip a day occasionally, assuring her that God wouldn't be displeased. In response, she blushed slightly, gazing at me, and shared, "Darling, God wouldn't be displeased regardless." She emphasized that her prayer was fueled by love for God rather than fear. To her, praying was akin to conversing with one of her own children. It was an activity she cherished, one that arose from her own genuine desire; no one forced or obligated her. She revealed that her habit of prayer began long before my birth. Each night, as she spent those moments in communion, she found strength for the coming day. Her prayers provided solace for the trials of each day, and most importantly, she experienced an overwhelming sense of peace.

She further explained that she didn't always have the strength to pray for extended periods every day. Some days, her prayers lasted merely five minutes, while on other nights, she might spend over an hour. It wasn't a mere routine; it was an integral part of her life. She shared that these prayerful moments were never a burden; she knew that God would always meet her, even before she sought Him. Regardless of her achievements during the day, the time she spent in prayer was the most beautiful and impactful part of her daily life. Remaining true to her words, every time I visited my hometown, I witnessed her dedication to personal prayer, a practice she upheld until she began to experience memory loss in her later years. Even during those challenging times, I am confident she continued her communion with Jesus, and in turn, He communicated with her.

Reflecting on my conversation with my grandmom, I recognized the immense significance of personal prayer. She lived to the age of 85, fulfilling roles as an exemplary daughter, devoted wife, loving mother, and nurturing grandmother. Her resilience and determination, I believe, were sourced from the divine. Those moments of quiet intimacy with Jesus each night provided her with the strength and vitality needed to embrace each day wholeheartedly. Despite the advice from my father and uncles, who sometimes cautioned her to rest and avoid straining herself, she persisted in her nightly prayers, revealing that prayer becomes burdensome only when it lacks authenticity. Prayer transforms into a passion when we cultivate a genuine relationship with the One, we are addressing—an endeavor that requires both time and effort.

Considering this realization, I resolved to dedicate a few minutes to personal prayer every day. My focus shifted away from the clock, and I accepted that some days I might manage only a moment, while other days I could linger longer. Slowly, I've been building my personal sanctuary with God, and I've begun to relish these moments. I've come to understand that even before I begin, Jesus is already present, awaiting my arrival.

As I conclude my personal prayers each day, I never fail to remember my beloved grandma. She taught me the essence of prayer and the value of patiently waiting in the presence of the Creator.

8. Marriage: Blessing or a Curse?

People say that different generations have different opinions and ideas about various things. One thing that has been changing a lot and is seen differently is marriage.

When I was young, I used to see my aunts and uncles getting married, and they all seemed happy and excited for a new life together. People around them spoke positively about building a strong relationship. But now, things have changed. When someone is about to get married, many people say negative things like "game over" or "it's the end."

But is marriage really the end of a good life?

Recently, I talked to a friend who was married and had a child. She told me she was unhappy and regretted getting married and having a child so early. This surprised me because her husband was a good man, and I never thought their marriage was bad. She explained that after having the baby, her husband suggested she take a break from work to take care of the child until they could find someone trustworthy to help. She felt upset being at home all the time and thought her marriage was the problem. I tried to help her understand that her husband was not wrong. He just wanted her to take care of herself and the baby for a while. But many of us today think marriage is bad just because we don't get everything we want. It's not about whether marriage itself is good or bad.

In the past, when we asked kids what they wanted to be when they grew up, many would say they wanted to get married. But now, if you ask kids, they often say they don't want to get married and waste their lives. This negative idea about marriage gets into their minds when they're young, and they end up having bad relationships when they grow up.

When I told my friends I would get married at 25, some of them laughed and made fun of me. They said my life was over and that I would just take care of my husband and kids. But that's not true. My marriage has been a wonderful journey. Yes, we've had our problems, fights, and tears like any couple, but we've also supported each other through everything. We've had amazing moments that we wouldn't have if we weren't married.

I asked some friends why they don't want to get married, and they said they see so many marriages failing that they don't want to end up unhappy. But the problem is not marriage itself; it's often because we choose the wrong person or don't try to be a good partner. Many young people expect too much from relationships and give up when things get a little tough.

I don't want to judge anyone, but I believe that most marriages can be saved with compromise, understanding, forgiveness, and love. Maybe we should be good examples for our kids and learn from our parents to have a strong and happy marriage.

No relationship is easy. Being a parent is hard; being a good friend takes effort; and so does keeping a strong bond with siblings. So why not put in that extra effort to keep a marriage strong?

I've always admired my parents, who have been together for many years and still love each other. They never complain about each other. Their love inspires me to have a similar marriage. Many of us today get influenced by the broken marriages we see in the media, which is a mistake. Instead, we should learn from successful marriages.

I'm not saying marriage is easy, but it's worth the effort. It might be the most challenging relationship, but it's also the most rewarding. Marriage has made me stronger and better at handling tough situations. I haven't given up my passions and dreams. My husband supports me and encourages me to pursue my goals. Most importantly, marriage has given me a best friend for life.

In this article, I want to highlight two important things. First, marriage is not bad or the end of happiness. It's the start of an exciting and fulfilling adventure. To make a marriage work, we need to put in effort. Sometimes we have to compromise and adjust, but it's all worth it when you love someone. Second, when choosing a life partner, we should be wise. Don't just look for looks, money, or wealth. Think about whether you can spend your life with that person. Let's choose someone who suits us and try to have a beautiful married life.

Next time a friend or relative is getting married, tell them how wonderful marriage can be. Create a positive environment so that young couples can start their marriage happily and keep it strong. This way, future generations will learn to respect and value the importance of marriage.

9. Growing Taller with "Magic" Sandals

Our world can be strange. Tall people sometimes want to be shorter, and short folks wish they were taller. Even those who are content with themselves still dream of improvements. I was like that too.

I'm not very tall. It's funny; I used to be the tallest in my family, school, and neighborhood until I was about 10 years old. But I guess I didn't realize there was a limit to how much I'd grow.

My height didn't bother me until my teenage years. When I turned sixteen, I felt a wave of inferiority. All my friends were taller and slimmer, looking like top models. I felt small and unnoticed.

That's when I decided I wanted to grow taller, no matter what it took. I tried skipping, walking, and jumping, but nothing seemed to work. I felt disappointed and downcast.

Then, one day while watching TV, I saw an ad for "magic" growth sandals. I knew exactly what to do. I watched the show every day, seeing young girls and boys grow 3 to 4 feet taller. It made me happy and excited. I believed I could grow taller too.

The next challenge was convincing my parents, which I knew would be hard. But I didn't give up. I kept trying day and night until, after several months, my parents finally agreed and gave their permission.

I called the person whose name always appeared on the TV screen during the ad. He was happy to talk to me. The very next day, he came up with the magical solution. It was a green mat that fit inside shoes and was supposed to help you grow taller when you walked on it daily. The "magic man" explained everything and showed pictures to my parents. He even brought a lady who had grown 3 inches taller at the age of 27. We were all excited. My dad gave him some money and handed me the magical item from the "magic man." I was overjoyed. The "magic man" measured my height by having me stand against a wall. He said I was 4.9 feet tall. Before leaving, he assured me that I would gain at least 3 inches within 6 months just by wearing the magical sandals and walking. He waved goodbye and left.

So, I began my mission. I got a nice pair of shoes and put the mat inside them. But the mat had sharp edges that hurt a lot. For a few days, it was tough to walk, and I even cried. But my determination to grow taller was stronger than the pain. I walked and walked for more than 6 months, but nothing seemed to change.

My parents scolded me, and my friends made fun of me. Feeling hurt by their teasing, I decided to check my height at a clinic. To my surprise, the doctor told me I was now 5 feet tall.

I was happy to have grown from 4.9 feet to 5 feet. I proudly walked home, but then I realized something odd. If I had really grown 3 inches, my clothes would have felt different. My sandals should have been tighter. But nothing had changed. How did I grow 3 inches then?

Feeling sad, I asked my parents if they noticed anything different about me. They said no. My dad even tried to call the "magic man," but his number wasn't working.

I gave up on getting taller. People around me sympathized with me. I was still puzzled about how I had grown. Almost a year later,

I found my school records. They showed my height from a year before the "magic man" came, and it was already 5 feet.

I realized I had been tricked. The "magic man" had lied about my height, so he could claim credit for any growth that happened.

Even now, 20 years later, I see ads on TV and elsewhere promising changes in appearance. It reminds me of the "magic man" and how I was deceived.

Today, I'm still 5 feet tall, not taller or shorter. But I've accepted myself as I am. Some things can't be changed.

We need to educate each other about fraudsters who make false claims. They say they can change our features, like eyes, hips, or noses. We might not be able to completely stop them, but we can make smart choices and warn others about their tricks. That way, we can help get rid of these dishonest people from our society.

I've kept those shoes as a reminder. Every time I look at them, I remember not to make the same mistakes and to embrace the things that can't be changed.

10. Good News

They say being a mother is the most wonderful experience and a special gift from God. Every woman dreams of holding her own baby and feeling the happiness that comes with it. But sometimes the path to motherhood can be tough. And whether we realize it or not, we all have a part to play in this.

When a couple gets married, the first question people often ask is, "When will you have a baby?" While having a baby is important, shouldn't we also celebrate other important moments in their journey? Their first trip together, moving into their own home, their accomplishments as a couple, and their love story—all these things are overshadowed. The beautiful process of becoming a mother is turned into a race where couples are compared to each other.

In many marriages, if there's a delay in getting pregnant, the woman is often blamed. But we need to understand that both partners need to be healthy for a pregnancy to happen. It's not fair to put all the pressure on the woman, making her feel sad and guilty.

Maybe the woman you're urging to have a baby has gone through many miscarriages. Perhaps she's tried different treatments and seen the best doctors. Is it really her fault that she can't get pregnant?

The young woman you keep asking for good news might have lost her first child and is still healing emotionally. Is it wrong for her to take time to recover?

The woman you're pressuring to see a doctor might be dealing with problems in her relationship that she's not ready to talk about. She might be silently suffering to avoid disappointing her husband.

The lady you're telling to have another child might not be ready. She might have decided to focus on her child with special needs, or she could be dealing with fears she doesn't share.

The woman you're making fun of for not having children might have gone through a serious illness. She might have lost her ability to have children because of a disease she didn't choose.

Society often expects a baby, but do we really understand that it takes time? Some couples become parents quickly, but for others, it's a longer journey. Sometimes, older generations say that young people avoid responsibility. While that might be true for some, it's not fair to say the same for all young couples. Deciding to become parents is something a couple should do together, so why does it become so difficult for many?

Because we're so focused on having a child, we often forget about the pain a woman goes through. In our society, we label a woman as barren and make fun of her, treating her as if she's not whole. Even though being a mother is wonderful, not having a child doesn't make her any less of a woman. We should value her as a loving wife, a caring daughter, and a great daughter-in-law. We should appreciate her skills and her career. She shouldn't be defined only by her ability to have children; that's not fair.

A woman who can't get pregnant for a long time goes through a lot. She feels guilty for disappointing her family and helpless when she sees her husband with other kids. Comparing her to other moms makes her smile, but it also hurts. Every time she sees a baby, she wonders what it's like to have her own. Baby showers and pregnancy announcements can be difficult for her. She faces all of this because of the pressure society puts on her.

I know this pain because I've been through it too. My husband and I have had miscarriages, and our journey hasn't been easy. Throughout it all, I've learned that, despite what society thinks, understanding and support from family can make a big difference.

Once, when I was feeling down about not getting pregnant, my husband's words touched me and changed how I saw things. He told me that children are a gift from God and that He will bless us when the time is right. He encouraged me to have faith and believe that we will have children, no matter what others say.

Whether we're parents, in-laws, friends, or family, the best thing we can do for couples waiting to have children is not to ask when they'll have good news. Instead, we can reassure them that good news will come and be patient. This change in how we approach things can bring comfort and strengthen their hope of becoming parents. Let's avoid judging couples without children; let's understand and support them on their journey to becoming parents. Let's also learn to appreciate a woman for all her qualities, not just her ability to have children. By doing this, we can bring hope and faith into someone's life.

Above all, let's remember that God has a plan. We should let His timing guide our lives instead of trying to force our own schedules on Him. Maybe then we'll find peace and happiness.

11. Ordinary Love

Parents are the most precious gift we receive. Their love, care, and concern are irreplaceable. They say a good parent teaches, but the best parent leads by example.

Like any child, I didn't truly appreciate my parents' value until I got married. Being the only child, I received lots of love and pampering. Yet, I was raised with discipline and was always an obedient daughter.

When I was with my parents, I never took the time to thank them or truly understand their upbringing's worth. I enjoyed a wonderful upbringing, got married, and entered family life.

Marriage and starting a family transform you, especially for women who adjust their personalities to fit the new family's needs. After marriage, I realized how it felt to give everything to a person—body, heart, and soul.

But like many young people, my understanding of love was flawed. We're in the age of WhatsApp, Twitter, Facebook, etc. Movies and TV shows emphasize expressing love verbally. Being married to a man who struggles with words (like many men), I felt our love was fading because he didn't say "I love you" often. I expected romantic gestures, surprises, chocolates, and flowers. When I didn't get them, I felt disappointed.

One day, feeling down, I looked at old photo albums and noticed my parents' wedding pictures. I wondered how they managed a happy life despite the ups and downs. This made me reflect on my own marriage. They'd been married for over 33 years, and yet I rarely heard my dad say "I love you" to my mom. I never saw flowers or chocolates. Yet they were in love.

Their love was in actions, not just words. I realized it was love when my tired dad helped my mom in the kitchen. It was love when he never complained about food and scolded me for criticizing mom's cooking. It was love when he did work without being asked. My mom's love showed when she managed to go home and work alone to support my dad. It was love when she brought home sweets my dad liked. Their love showed in respect, in happy conversations, and in supporting each other.

I understood what love was. I was happy because I was in love. My husband's actions revealed his love: he appreciates me, supports me, and changes plans for me. He switches off Netflix to talk to me. His hard work secures our future. He's jealous when other men look at me. He holds my hand and wakes up for me. He can't bear my tears. We eat, pray, and laugh together. He respects and encourages me.

I realized the true meaning of love. Marriage is a beautiful journey with ups and downs that is worth living.

My parents gave me much, but the greatest gift is their example. Their love taught me life lessons. A man's greatest gift to his child is loving their mother, as my dad showed. My parents set standards: love isn't just flowers or gifts. Love is action.

Many of us aren't happy due to unrealistic expectations. Let's appreciate what we have, not what we lack. Actions speak louder. When your spouse forgets flowers but gives a tight hug, be happy—you're lucky. Treasure what you have.

12. Exploring Kerala: A Humorous Night in a Tree House

Apart from enjoying writing, reading, and music, I really like traveling. Ever since I was a kid, I've been super excited about finding new places, understanding how people live there, and getting to know their different cultures.

Because my parents had jobs, it was tough to take time off for trips, so I couldn't explore new places like I wanted. Every year, the only trip I took was back to my hometown, Mangalore, a beautiful city in Karnataka, India. I always looked forward to this yearly trip.

In college, there weren't many planned trips. Even though my friends and I made a lot of plans, none of them happened. But like they say, good things come to those who wait. Just when I thought I might never get to travel to new places, I married a man who loved traveling and adventures too. Within four months of getting married, we had already been to two places and were planning our third trip. I picked the place, but we both decided on things like the budget and travel dates. After waiting for this chance for so long, I could only think of one place: Kerala, often called "God's Own Country."

Even though my husband had been to Kerala before and wasn't very excited about going again, he agreed to make me happy. I was so happy! I wanted this trip to be the best because it was making a dream come true that I had had for years. (I had tried to go to Kerala twice before this, but it didn't work out.) I spent a lot of my free time looking for places to visit, good hotels, and yummy restaurants.

After thinking carefully, I booked a place to stay that had a tent experience and a day in a tree house. We also planned to spend the last day on a houseboat.

The thing I was most excited about was the tree house. Every day, I looked at pictures online, showed them to my friends, and talked about them with my husband. He wasn't sure about my choice, but he didn't want to disappoint me.

Finally, the day came to pack our bags and start our journey. We got on a bus and went to Kerala. The ride to the place we were staying was bumpy and a little scary because the road was rough and hilly. We felt both excited and nervous. When we got to the place, we were surprised. It was beautiful and far away from the city. There were only the people who worked there and visitors like us. I was proud of my choice when we went into our tents. They were nice, but I couldn't wait to see the treehouse.

After spending a day in the tent, we explored the town and came back in the evening. We were happy when we found out we were going to stay in the tree house. There were five tree houses. Four were close together, and the fifth was a bit farther away. We got the fifth one, which was more private.

Our tree house was amazing. It was made of wood and had a big bed in the middle. There were tables and chairs that made it perfect. It felt special to be up in a tree. I loved looking at the view. As the sun went down and the stars came out, I noticed something different. It was very quiet, and I couldn't hear cars or people like I was used to. I only heard the trees rustling and my husband's voice. This was so different from the busy city life in Bangalore, where there's always noise from cars and people. Even though I thought my husband felt the same, I didn't say anything because of my pride.

After dinner, we sat on the balcony and looked at the dark night before going to sleep. But we couldn't sleep. It was too quiet, and we felt alone. We tried to listen to music, talk, and even look at our wedding photos on our phones, but nothing helped us fall asleep. Finally, we decided to have a drink in the hope that it would make us sleepy. But that didn't work either. After a struggle that lasted until almost 2 in the morning, we were so tired that we fell asleep. Just then, I heard something that sounded like footsteps on the ceiling.

It surprised me, and I moved closer to my husband, who was still awake. He asked me what was wrong, but I didn't say anything. I looked away and didn't want to look at the door or the windows. I started thinking strange things, wondering if it could be a ghost or someone trying to break in. I remembered what my friends said about ghosts living in trees. I felt really scared and didn't know what to do. I thought about all the ghost movies I had watched and imagined what kind of ghost could be in our tree house. I wanted to scream and cry, so I woke up my husband and asked him to pray, hoping to chase the ghost away. I played music too, but the noise just got louder. I was surprised that my husband wasn't doing anything. I was almost crying, and I finally fell asleep when it was starting to get light outside.

In the morning, we got up, got dressed, and wanted to leave for our next stop. Neither of us wanted to talk about what happened the night before.

As we sat in the car and drove to our next destination, I casually asked my husband if he feared ghosts. He said no, which made me happy. I told him that's why he hadn't reacted to the noises last night. He asked me why I was so scared, so I told him that there was a ghost in the tree we stayed in, and it was making noise all night.

He started laughing! He asked why I didn't tell him earlier. I said I didn't want to scare him. He laughed and explained that the noise wasn't a ghost but just birds in the trees. I felt really embarrassed. I had stayed awake the whole night, thinking there was a ghost on the tree. I laughed at myself and couldn't even look at my husband.

I'll never forget what happened in the tree house. Even now, when we talk about it, I can't help but laugh at how silly I was. My husband still makes fun of me, and my friends think it's funny too. This experience taught me that we often have problems because we don't talk openly. If I had told my husband, I would have known it was just birds, and I wouldn't have missed a good night's sleep.

This story is funny, but it also reminds me, and it should remind all of you, that we should always be open in our relationships. When we share our thoughts and feelings with the people we love, it helps us and makes our relationships stronger.

In the end, even though the trip didn't go exactly as I hoped, I have a memory that I'll never forget.

13. Home Maker?

Recently, while browsing, I came across a wonderful article discussing a study conducted by the Organization for Economic Cooperation and Development (OECD) in 2011. It stated that the average Indian woman spent nearly six hours a day doing unpaid housework. Economists believed that, though unpaid, the household work done by homemakers constituted economic activity and should be included in the national income. By ignoring it, we were underestimating women's contribution to the economy.

Having completed college, my very next thought was to get a job. Unlike others, I did not want any breaks, and my only goal was to be employed. Looking back, I realize that my urgency to work was probably not for the joy of working but to avoid being labeled as unemployed by society.

I'm sure most of us have gone through this phase, and for women, it's a bigger challenge as they have many milestones to overcome to be employed. Even today, some families are unwilling to accept a working woman and label it as a man's job. For women, it is considered a hobby to be pursued at their convenience.

My topic for today is slightly different, and I want to focus on those ladies who wholeheartedly choose to stay at home and become homemakers despite having competent degrees and educational qualifications. Our society is shifting paradigms. There was a time when working women were considered taboo, but today we have come to a point where a woman choosing to stay at home is considered lazy and without a goal.

My thoughts regarding this concept were not very clear, and I was constantly baffled by innumerable contradicting arguments. Having been brought up in a family where my mother was a working woman, I realized how wonderfully a woman can manage work and home without giving a reason to complain. After marriage, I was again with two ladies, my mother-in-law and sister-in-law, who, despite being married and in good positions at work, managed both work and the household meticulously. Somewhere in my mind, I had decided that being a working woman was better than staying at home.

But life, they say, has a different way of throwing things at your feet, and sometimes you are forced to step on them without any option. The same happened to me. After six long years of a successful career as a lecturer and then as an HR professional, there came a point where I had to quit and stay at home for a few months due to a personal issue. I was not sure; I was in a dilemma. The fear of financial dependency scared me, and the boredom and anxiety of losing my identity filled my mind. I had no option; half-heartedly, I decided to quit my job and stay at home.

There were a lot of raised eyebrows, and many people suggested that I could juggle work and home and that I had made a cowardly decision. Some went on to say that I was lazy and did not want to work, so I stayed at home to lead a luxurious life. All that said and done, when I stayed at home, that's when I realized how much work a homemaker does. From cooking, cleaning, and doing laundry to dishes and grocery shopping, everything is expected from a homemaker. She is expected to do everything and ask for nothing in return. This phase of my life answered all the questions in my mind, and I began to understand that a homemaker also utilizes her skills like any working professional.

The only difference is that working women may extensively use one skill, whereas a homemaker uses numerous skills. The most important aspect is appreciation and recognition. In most cases, a working woman receives recognition in the form of a monetary return, but in all cases, a homemaker's work is neither recognized nor monetarily rewarded.

A few years ago, the Women and Child Development Minister, Krishna Tirath, suggested that the invisible labor performed by homemakers should be quantified and that they should be paid by their husbands. He suggested values such as Rs 6,000 for cooking, Rs 3,000 for housekeeping, Rs 4,000 for accounting, Rs 12,000 for taking care of kids, etc. Though this bill was never passed, it gives insight that the work done by women is valuable, and staying at home does not make a woman less competitive or lazy. In fact, a woman who stays at home works from morning until night.

I started realizing how much sacrifice a woman who stays at home makes. Most of the women who stay at home may not like to do so, but the situation and realities of life force them to, and yet they accept their role lovingly without cribbing and complaining. Recent studies suggest that many women who stay at home suffer from insecurity and depression. Not because they are unoccupied, but because they are made to feel inferior by the people around them, failing to understand the true value of their work. Most Indian households still follow the stereotypical approach that if anything happens in the family, then it is the woman's responsibility to stay at home and take care, while a man continues his career. In such a scenario, we must salute all those ladies who do not think twice and give up their careers, dreams, and passions for the betterment of their spouses and family.

Studies reveal that even though housework may seem routine, it involves a lot of mental and emotional stress. Women tend to spend considerable amounts of time not just working but also planning and executing, much like any professional working for an organization.

After staying at home, I started realizing no job was easy, and every state of living that a woman chooses involves a lot of hard work.

Having played both roles, I equally admire those working women who work double shifts. Every working woman finishes one shift at her workplace and then returns home to continue her second shift without a moment of rest. If staying at home and taking care of the house is a tedious job, then working and taking care are equally challenging. A big salute to all those women who play this dual role with perfection and ease.

In conclusion, I realized that staying at home was not a crime. The misconceptions and prejudices in my mind vanished, and I realized that whether I am working or choose to continue to stay at home and take care of the family, my value will never be defined by it. My value will be based on the work I do, the happiness I spread, and the value I add to society.

After a few months' break, I returned to work, but with a difference. If the need arises for me to quit my job and stay at home for any reason, I would do so boldly and proudly, without fearing my value or worth. Maybe it's time to let the women around us make their decisions. If a woman chooses to stay at home and dedicate her time to family and kids, then appreciate her. If another woman chooses to work and take care of the family, then support her, but never judge her actions and label her where she does not belong.

As a society, let's learn to respect the decisions made by those around us, irrespective of gender. Perhaps it's time for us to break prejudices, delve deep, reflect on the reasons behind the decisions those around us make, and appreciate them for the little sacrifices they make without the knowledge of many.

14. He Taught Me to Smile

Every day is tough for a woman who works. You wake up early, make breakfast for the family, get things ready, and rush to work. In the evening, you come back, finish chores, and then go to sleep. Time moves quickly, and we often forget to smile, relax, and unwind. The world is changing, and the people around us hesitate to greet us with a smile and a friendly hello, making us wonder why.

My story is almost the same. I wake up early every day and hurry to work. Work is a new challenge each day. Some days go smoothly, while others are difficult to understand.

One Thursday, in the middle of the week, I woke up late. I rushed to work without cooking anything, leaving instructions for my husband to fend for himself. Breakfast was just some humble oats, and I had to take care of lunch. My time at the office was busy. My boss scolded me, and I was bombarded with tasks. Amidst all this, my hunger grew, and I quickly ordered food online and continued working.

Until the afternoon, I walked around with a grumpy face and avoided talking to anyone. After almost 40 minutes, I realized my food hadn't arrived. I checked my phone and saw that the delivery person had come. I peeped out of my workspace and saw an old, short, thin man holding my parcel. I immediately recognized him and rushed to get my food.

I was angry with him and chose to ignore and reject him. But despite my rude behavior, he apologized to me. He told me he had been waiting for about 3 minutes. I asked him why he hadn't called me. He responded with a gentle smile and explained that he saw everyone in the office was busy, so he didn't want to disturb me. He had left a message for me, letting me know about his arrival. He remained calm, smiled, and asked me to give him a rating based on my satisfaction before leaving the office with a big smile.

There was something about this man that really moved me. In that moment, my cluttered thoughts and anger seemed to quiet down, and I began to think about him. Normally, when I order food, the delivery people rush due to a 10-minute limit to deliver, or they get charged for parking. Most of them start calling from the elevator and get annoyed if we're even 2 minutes late picking up the parcel from the door. This man, around 50 years old, was so kind and considerate. He didn't mind the parking fee; he valued my time. He smiled, and even after my rudeness, he continued to smile and politely asked for a rating of his service according to my judgment.

This man's character truly amazed me. He wasn't highly educated and didn't work in a fancy office; he wandered the city delivering food for others. He was polite and put in his best effort at his job, always with a smile. Looking at him, I realized the significance of a smile. A terrible day turned into a better one, and I learned a lifelong lesson from his simplicity, honesty, and that big, wide smile.

I couldn't do much, but I gave him a generous tip for his excellent work ethic and thanked him wholeheartedly. This simple man taught me to diligently perform my tasks despite challenges, and above all, he taught me the value of a smile.

15. A Tale of Mother's Love

As their only child, I was the focus of my parents' lives. Everything they did revolved around my happiness. I was very close to my dad and loved both my parents equally. While my mom was strict, my dad was gentler. His stern look could make me cry, unlike mom's scolding. I enjoyed a wonderful childhood with their care and support.

On one side, there was me, and on the other, there was the strong bond between my parents. They are the couple I look up to as role models. Dad always helped mom, even anticipating her needs. He aimed to make things easy for her so she wouldn't struggle. Mom, on the other hand, managed work and home perfectly, never complaining.

Relatives and friends envied my mom, labeling her fragile because she seemed dependent on dad. They talked about how she'd manage without him. I never thought she was weak, but I did wonder how she'd cope without dad's help.

After about two and a half years of marriage, I got pregnant. This was a dream my parents had cherished for a long time. They eagerly awaited their grandchild's arrival. Things were going well. Mom started preparing, collecting clothes, and arranging for a caretaker.

However, on a fateful morning, things took a turn. I experienced intense stomach pain and backache. I was rushed to the hospital. Up until then, everything had been fine. I was three months and twenty days into the pregnancy, with dreams and hopes for my little one.

I remember being in excruciating pain, lying in the hospital bed. One face was with me all the time, holding my hands—my mother's. She stood by me as I cried in pain and desperation, when I began bleeding, when the doctors couldn't detect the baby's heartbeat, and when I was told my baby was gone. She stayed strong, not showing her own grief. When I blamed myself and wondered why, she held me tight and reassured me that everything would be okay.

Even though she wanted to hold my baby just as much, she didn't let a tear fall. She didn't want me to feel worse. My husband and dad were outside, crying, and lost. But my mom, whom some called weak, stood by me like a rock. I struggled for five hours, and she stood with me, supporting me. Even after I was discharged and came home, she didn't cry or blame anyone. She cared for me, managed the house, and made sure I was safe.

This incident made me realize my mom's strength, patience, and incredible abilities. She was going through her own turmoil, yet she stayed calm and supported me, my dad, and my husband. I'm sure she cried outside, but whenever she faced me, she stayed calm. My dad and husband were at a loss for what to do, while this so-called "weak" woman stood strong by my side, handling everything.

That day, I truly understood my mom's strength and gained a newfound respect for her. I had always loved her, but from that moment on, my admiration took on a new dimension. She's the kind of woman I aspire to be. She's not into flashy things, fancy phones, or fluent English. She doesn't attend parties or join clubs. But she's a woman of class and dignity. She's a perfect mother, and her love for her child is priceless. Even now, when the world asks about my plans for having a child, she doesn't pressure me. She advises me to recover fully, both physically and emotionally, displaying her selfless love.

They say God does everything for the good of His people. While losing my child was heartbreaking, it taught me so much. It made me stronger, helped me understand the value of those around me, and showed me the true essence of motherhood.

16. The Power of Apologies

At some point in our lives, we all think back to our childhood and remember how wonderful it was. As we grow older, our egos, pride, and self-centeredness also grow.

We tend to forget the innocence, the fun, the laughter, and the importance of letting go.

The teenage years are often seen as difficult. There's confusion, a search for identity, and a strong desire for freedom. Many people complain about today's teenagers, comparing them to their own younger days. I disagree. I think today's teenagers are challenging, but they're open-minded and have a perspective on life we could learn from.

One day, after work, I got on the bus to go home. The journey usually takes about half an hour. I spend my time either looking out the window if I get a seat or waiting for someone to leave so I can take their seat.

On that day, I was in a bad mood because I had argued with someone close to me. We weren't speaking to each other. At first, we argued a couple of times, but things were slowly getting back to normal, except for the fact that we weren't talking. We had been close for a long time and had wonderful memories together. But this silence was hurting both of us. I wanted to resolve the issue, but I didn't know how.

I didn't want to be the first to start talking, as it would hurt my pride. And she didn't want to either. I hoped she would approach me, but she was even more stubborn than I was. This situation left me confused, and I just stared out of the window, lost in thought.

Suddenly, I overheard a conversation between two young college girls sitting behind me. Usually, the bus is noisy with college students talking about their teachers, movies, or clothes. I usually put on my earphones to block out the noise. But this conversation was different. I was curious to listen because they seemed to be resolving an argument. One of the girls was upset and was accusing the other of betraying her. The other girl stayed quiet, and then she said, "I am sorry; please forgive me and let's be how we were." The upset girl replied angrily, "Sorry cannot bring the dead man alive." This phrase reminded me of my childhood, when we used it to show frustration. I was curious about the other girl's response. I had to get off the bus soon, so I was eager to hear what she'd say. It was like watching a movie and reaching the most exciting part. Finally, the quiet girl said, "I know my sorry cannot bring the dead man alive, but it can definitely bring back the love and friendship we had."

I was amazed by her mature reply. My stop arrived, and as I got off, I looked at the girl, who was about 16 or 17 years old. She seemed plain, but her calmness and patience left me speechless.

I don't know what happened next. I still don't know if they stayed friends or went their separate ways. But that conversation taught me a lot.

Realizing that I was almost losing a precious friendship, I decided it was time to apologize. I didn't know how things would turn out. I didn't know if we would become close again. The outcome was uncertain, but I knew I would be happy that I tried my best to mend things.

That night, after dinner, I gathered my courage and sent a message saying, "I am so sorry. Please forgive me if I have hurt you." I sent the message, and, to my delight, I got a reply saying, "It's okay. I am sorry too. Let's be friends again."

I was overjoyed. Just a simple apology brought us back together. I felt grateful to those girls. Their conversation taught me the importance of apologizing sincerely.

How many of us have lost precious relationships due to our pride? How many of us can't forgive and forget? Apologizing may not fix everything, but it will heal you. The guilt, shame, and helplessness will disappear because you'll know you did your best, and that's what matters most.

If you want to reconcile with someone today, just send a text and say sorry. You never know; the other person might also be hesitant, waiting to make amends. Let's leave the past behind and look forward to a fresh start filled with positivity.

17. Drive Away Your Mind

We live in a world where there's often pressure to conform to society's norms and expectations. While it's true that we all live within society and should follow its rules, it's not necessary to always go along with the crowd and measure your value solely based on society's standards.

I've faced various challenges, and one thing that some people in society have pointed out is that I don't know how to drive. I did have a desire to learn, but circumstances and situations during my teenage years didn't allow for it.

I faced criticism and received comments; some people even laughed and thought I lacked courage. However, I chose to overlook these comments and keep moving forward. Despite dealing positively with these rude remarks, I encountered yet another comment, this time from a family member. He often made fun of me, which I tolerated, but every situation has a limit. On a casual day when I met him, he teased me and suggested I could use his vehicle to go somewhere. I didn't respond, but he continued, saying, "You don't know how to drive? Hasn't your father taught you? That's disappointing. I taught my daughter to drive."

These remarks ignited a desire within me to respond. I politely told him that my dad hadn't taught me how to drive a car, but he had taught me something equally valuable—the ability to travel independently. My father encouraged me to use public transportation fearlessly and instilled the courage to explore various places on my own, without fearing anything or anyone. My dad had taught me to be independent and manage even without a vehicle. His teachings made me capable of moving around without relying on anyone or anything. Having my own vehicle wouldn't make a difference to me because I knew I could get by without one.

After saying this, I realized that my response had unsettled him. He had focused solely on teaching his daughter to drive, neglecting to teach her the courage to explore boldly. I was content because, even though I couldn't drive a vehicle, I had influenced his mindset.

Many of us encounter situations where people mock us for not being perfect. Some people enjoy pointing out others' weaknesses while ignoring their own flaws. Let's not let these comments drain us, but rather, let's learn to accept them positively. When you feel the need to do something, do it. But if you don't think it's necessary, forget about it. Don't do things solely to gain society's approval; do them because you genuinely want to.

I know that I'll eventually learn to drive and navigate the roads. However, I'm not in a rush to please anyone. Until then, I'll happily explore the busy streets of Bangalore using buses, autos, and walking. So, the next time you question me, I might drive your mind away.

18. The Prize That Surprised Me

I'm sure we all agree that childhood days are the best part of life. It doesn't matter which school we attended or how we studied; every memory is treasured. I went to a convent school, and everything there was well organized. The school's atmosphere instilled in me a sense of discipline, commitment, and love for learning.

While I never aimed to top the class, I always intended to excel in whatever I pursued. One thing I wished for during my school days was to win trophies. The catch was that I wasn't into sports at all. In fact, I almost disliked sports and only occasionally tried my hand at things like basketball and shot put. However, I did well in cultural activities and earned many certificates, but a trophy remained elusive.

I truly wanted a trophy; I was tired of certificates and medals. However, I knew my chances were dwindling as I approached the end of my school years. I was already thinking about how I could win trophies in college when I received news: I had secured the 8th rank in the Bangalore Diocese catechism exams, which were for Catholic students across the city. I was happy with my achievement, but even more so because I had seen senior students who ranked well in these exams being awarded trophies.

I was overjoyed. I was eagerly awaiting the day of the felicitation. After some waiting, it was announced in the assembly that there would be a function the following week to honor the winners and rank holders. My happiness knew no bounds. The days leading up to it were hard to get through, and I couldn't sleep at night.

Finally, the day came. I made sure my uniform was neatly ironed, and I dressed up for the occasion. I sat in the front row of the auditorium with pride, eagerly waiting for the speeches to end. Then, the moment I had been waiting for arrived: names were called, and each person who excelled in various fields received a beautiful trophy. I couldn't take my eyes off those trophies, especially the glass ones with the school's name etched on them. Everyone got their trophies, and then they announced that the students who ranked well in catechism would be honored. When my name was called first, I walked proudly to the stage, only to be handed a gift wrapped in golden paper instead of a trophy. I was shocked and sad. This wasn't how it was supposed to be; they had always given trophies in the past. Tears welled up in my eyes. I felt let down.

I took the gift and walked back to my seat after the ceremony. Others were congratulating me, but I didn't respond. I went back to my place, fighting back tears. Then, the catechism teacher approached me, wished me well, and told me there was a beautiful surprise inside the gift. She said it was something I'd treasure forever.

I was furious. I thought it was probably a book, and I wasn't interested in opening it. I had planned to keep only the certificate and toss the gift away. I put it in my bag, and I spent the whole day in silent tears. When I got home, I took the gift out to throw it away, and my mom asked what it was. I didn't want to open it, but I also didn't want to show how much the trophy had meant to me. Reluctantly, I unwrapped it and was surprised to find a Holy Bible. I was conflicted; I didn't know what to do. Since we already had a couple of Bibles, I put them away. I was angry for many days, angry at the school, the management, and everyone who'd chosen a Bible over a trophy.

Years went by; I graduated and started my post-graduation. I hadn't completely forgotten about the trophy incident, but I had grown enough to realize that dwelling on it was pointless. One day, as I sat quietly and pulled open a drawer to get my diary, my eyes fell on the Bible. It looked untouched and neat after seven years. Something urged me to pick it up. At that time, I was navigating the confusions of adolescence, identity crises, and struggles with self-worth. That's when the Bible caught my attention. I opened it and was thrilled to read a paragraph congratulating me on my rank. After seven years, I finally read the message, and it made me happy. It motivated me.

Gradually, I began reading the Bible daily; it became my personal Bible. I started underlining the words that resonated with me. It became my close companion over the years. Even now, I still have that Bible. I read it every day. Whenever I'm feeling down, demotivated, frustrated, or angry, it's been my source of comfort and guidance. The gift I once despised has become my strongest source of support.

When I look back on that incident, I realize how foolish I was to chase after something so materialistic. Since then, I've won many trophies, including a gold medal, but nothing brings me as much comfort as the Bible does. All those medals and certificates are behind me.

Today, I understand the value of the gift I received. If I had gotten a trophy back then, it might have ended up in a showcase with little meaning. The Bible, on the other hand, made a significant impact on my life.

Many times, we get frustrated when we receive something we don't want. But maybe we should remember that God gives us what we truly need and deserve. Whatever we receive will surely help us in the future, even if we don't realize it at the time. No gift is useless. Let's cherish the gifts we receive and hold onto them with pride and love.

19. Embracing a Pause

As we grow up, we learn some basic rules for life. We're told to study well, get degrees, and find high-paying jobs. Nowadays, it's important for both men and women to have successful careers. Women now have more freedom to pause their careers when they become mothers. Unlike in the past, women are no longer forced to stay at home. In today's growing economy, having a job and a successful career are expected.

This is a great change, and it's motivating. I had been part of the daily grind for almost 9 years, but then I decided to step back and take a break from my stable job.

There wasn't a specific reason. I just wanted to take some time off.

Was it an easy decision? Definitely not! Despite what others thought, I was personally torn. I had been working since right after finishing my education, even through tough times and major life events. Taking a break for no clear reason was unsettling. Plus, I was worried about missing out on opportunities and facing criticism from society. Most importantly, I didn't like the idea of depending solely on my husband financially. However, after thinking deeply, I left my job and transitioned from being a career woman to taking care of my home.

The first few months were challenging. Family members asked uncomfortable questions and gave me strange looks. The only excuse

I could come up with was that I was taking a break to focus on myself and writing, even though that wasn't entirely true.

In a casual chat, a friend asked me, "So, what did you do during these six months? Did you learn to drive? Finish a novel? Travel?" I was caught off guard! I had to pause and really think about what I had accomplished in the last six months. I didn't have a satisfying answer, so I avoided the question.

Later, I realized that I hadn't achieved much during those six months. I had written a few articles and managed my home, but that was about it. Surprisingly, I felt fine about it. I hadn't learned to dance, drive, or go on big adventures. I hadn't even lost weight. Yet, I wasn't upset. I was content. I had learned to relax. I embraced taking care of my home and found joy in simple tasks. On cold days, I slept a bit more, and on tough nights, I stayed up later. I felt relieved not to have work calls, targets, or the need to impress anyone. This break was a chance to step away from my old self.

It's not a rule that a break must involve learning or achieving. It varies for each person. This break gave me the chance to reconsider parts of my life I had ignored. I had time to think, contemplate, and meditate. I reconnected with my spiritual side, and most importantly, I recharged.

This writing isn't about urging people to quit jobs and stay home. It's for those who keep working because of societal pressure. It's okay to take a break if you want to. It's fine if you don't check off anything from your to-do list during the break. A break is about you. It's your choice, and you have every right to make it.

After almost six months of a break, I was more focused on my goals. This pause had given me energy to pursue what I wanted. If you're thinking of taking a break without a clear reason, don't worry. Relax, enjoy your moments, and when you're truly ready, bounce back into your career!

20. Journey from Scars to Stars: My Path After Recurrent Miscarriages

Growing up as an only child, I never experienced life's struggles. I was fortunate to have loving parents, a wonderful upbringing, and the best facilities imaginable. Despite being the center of my parents' world, they taught me empathy, mutual love, and discipline.

I was blessed with a wonderful husband who loved and encouraged me to be my best. It was beautiful, and yes, I lived a fairytale life.

After two years of marriage, we decided to start a family and have a baby. Little did I know that this journey would be so challenging. After eight long months of trying, I became pregnant. This news was incredibly joyful for both me and my husband. As first-time parents-to-be, we were cautious and took all precautions to ensure the well-being of our unborn child.

Due to my heavier weight, I was always mindful of its potential impact on the baby. I read a lot about how weight could affect the unborn child, leading to constant caution and concern.

The first three months of pregnancy passed relatively smoothly, despite bouts of terrible nausea. However, one Saturday morning in the fourth month of my pregnancy, for reasons unknown, I experienced a miscarriage. This was a devastating blow to me. The months that followed were not easy. While my physical healing was quick, my emotional healing was painfully slow. Eventually, I managed to recover and resume my previous lifestyle.

My lifestyle wasn't praiseworthy; it consisted of junk food, a lack of exercise, and a lack of spiritual connection. This pattern continued for a couple of months. Suddenly, societal pressures mounted for us to have a baby. That's when I realized I needed to shed the excess weight I was carrying. Unfortunately, my lack of dedication, along with societal norms regarding my age and other criteria, left me in a dilemma. Ultimately, I made up my mind to take my weight loss goals seriously, and I became pregnant again.

Although this was good news, it brought about conflicting feelings. I was determined to lose weight, and pregnancy meant halting those goals. Nevertheless, with a strong heart, I embraced the pregnancy and gave it my best effort. With a history of miscarriage, I was advised to follow strict bed rest, a protein-rich diet, injections, medications, and more. Despite these efforts, I experienced another miscarriage in the fifth month. It was a heartbreaking experience for me and my family.

Amid sympathetic voices and critical opinions, one comment blamed my weight for the losses. It hurt, and I blamed myself. However, after a conversation with my doctor, I was reassured that my weight wasn't the cause. Despite this assurance, I knew I needed to take things seriously and make lifestyle changes.

The journey following the miscarriages was challenging, yet it held its own beauty. I learned many important life lessons.

I understood that miscarriage wasn't God's plan. Although many said I should accept it as God's plan, I realized it was the devil's work, and I needed to resist it. I decided to face the situation with faith and seek the support of a higher power. I learned that it was okay to talk about miscarriage, but not in a negative light. I learned to communicate with other women and share the message that miracles happen and that nothing is impossible for the almighty.

I began treating my body with respect. Our bodies are temples of God, and we should care for them physically and emotionally. Most importantly, I learned not to base my decisions on others' opinions but to pray for guidance and act accordingly.

The days following the miscarriage were not easy, marked by aches, pains, and frustrations. However, I gradually started to heal. I turned to reading the Bible, listening to the word of God, and spending time in prayer. These practices became the best remedy for my wounded heart. Strengthening my relationship with God made me realize that miscarriage wasn't His will but rather the devil's evil design. I also realized that when we have faith in Him, things change and miracles occur.

Furthermore, I committed to taking my weight-loss goals seriously. Although my weight had nothing to do with the miscarriages, I recognized the importance of treating my body with respect and maintaining a healthy lifestyle. Regardless of how many months it would take or who would be disappointed, I was determined to shed the excess weight and become a healthy mom. I started taking small steps, and the results began to show. I am confident that I will soon be able to shed the excess weight.

Additionally, I chose to write about taboo issues. Previously diplomatic, I realized the importance of addressing everything, particularly issues close to my heart. I started writing about both sad and happy topics, empowering myself and giving a voice to issues that are often ignored.

Although many saw my loss as a tragedy, I began to realize that my scars were transforming into bright stars, comforted by Jesus.

While losing a baby was incredibly difficult, the days that followed held promise. I started changing my unhealthy lifestyle and moving toward a healthier one. I pursued my interests and, most importantly, began trusting and relying on a higher power. While God might be viewed as fiction by some, my miscarriage transformed Him into a reality for me. My spiritual journey filled me with hope and joy, giving me a reason to live and love once again!

21. Sailing Through Storms: A Tale about Coping and Love

Life brings both the familiar and the unexpected. We navigate routine situations with ease through preparation, finding solace in predictability. But when life surprises us with challenges, coping becomes exhausting and heartbreaking.

Following marriage, I encountered numerous unforeseen circumstances. With the unwavering support of my husband, I gracefully navigated these trials. It wouldn't be inaccurate to say that we faced them together. Financial hardships, work-related stress, differing expectations, and family conflicts—we confronted them all. Through divine favor, we emerged as a resilient couple, even amid these trying times.

Among these challenges, one situation proved particularly difficult: our pregnancy loss. After two years of marriage, I experienced the joy of pregnancy for the first time. Surrounding us was an air of celebration, with excitement radiating from everyone, including ourselves. Despite our underlying fears and uncertainties, we embraced the journey ahead.

The bliss was short-lived; after four months, a miscarriage shattered our happiness. The news devastated those around me. Sympathy messages flowed from friends and relatives, while my family and friends were weighed down by sorrow. Once discharged, I returned home to unwavering support from my parents, particularly my mother, who dedicated herself to my care. Yet nights posed a challenge.

At 27, I learned what true sleeplessness felt like. Each night, I lay awake, unable to sleep or even cry. Staring into emptiness, I found myself unable to engage in any activity. My husband noticed this, becoming a steadfast presence. He spoke to me, even staying awake with me throughout the night. Our conversations, not tethered to any topic, offered solace.

Throughout the day, I lacked motivation for anything. Taking a break from work, I had no interest in conversation, movies, or writing. Time seemed suspended, much like my nights.

After several restless and sleepless days, my husband suggested we watch a movie instead of aimlessly staying awake. Though I was hesitant, knowing he shared my pain encouraged me to agree.

That night, my husband set up the laptop in bed, ready for our movie night. To my surprise, he had chosen "Pirates of the Caribbean," a movie I had previously attempted to watch but didn't quite enjoy. Despite this, my husband insisted I give it another chance. After some initial reluctance, I agreed. As the movie progressed, I found myself getting more involved and eventually enjoying it. I laughed—something I hadn't done in days. Gradually, conversations with my husband took a positive turn.

This trend continued, and we discussed nothing but the movies. The distraction provided by the movies didn't erase the pain, but it provided respite for my mind. Sleep returned, and I resumed my routine, stepping back into my old life.

Hindsight showed me that my husband had chosen an unconventional way to deal with our grief. Recognizing that discussing it would intensify my pain and staying silent would worsen things, he decided to divert my attention with a movie I initially had no interest in.

I realized that every couple finds their own unique approach to managing stress. Some may choose a getaway to unwind, while others might seek the support of friends and family. Each couple finds their escape—a way to overcome tragedy and begin anew.

As the years passed in our marriage, my husband and I developed our ways of coping with stress and adversity. Our journey wasn't without further challenges. Alongside additional pregnancy losses and health problems, we faced them head-on, armed with prayers and faith.

Through it all, I learned that even the most profound tragedies can be conquered with love, support, and dedication. I'm still amazed by my husband's unwavering strength during my times of disappointment and loss. He stood by me, devising ways to navigate our challenges gracefully. In any marriage, it's essential to support one another, hand in hand, as we navigate life's storms.

22. A Simple "Thank You"

Cooking is enjoyed by many. For some, it's a passion; for others, it's a necessity. Traditionally, women are expected to learn cooking for happiness, though this trend is shifting. Men are now also prominent in the kitchen, including in India, where some culinary giants are male.

In the traditional setup, women are often the ones expected to cook. I enjoyed cooking, and more than that, watching others cook. My parents often grew annoyed that, given the chance, I'd watch cooking shows 24/7. I dreamed of becoming a chef and collected recipes.

In my family, it was a blessing that women were excellent cooks. My working mother always prepared delicious and unique meals. She never followed TV or books; she followed her method, always serving something yummy.

What bothered me more than my mother's cooking was my father's reaction. For over 30 years, I've seen him appreciate her cooking. Even when dishes turned out spicy or bland, my dad always said it was the best meal ever.

This irritated me; I believed in giving honest feedback. Even though I complained, my dad discouraged me. I asked him why he wasn't critical, and he said I'd understand after marriage.

After my marriage, cooking became my responsibility. My husband had grown up enjoying meals made by my skilled mom-in-law. Our cooking styles differed, and comparisons were inevitable.

I was lucky to have an undemanding husband. He appreciated my cooking rarely but never complained. Initially, I enjoyed cooking, but it soon felt burdensome, and I cooked out of obligation.

One day, tired and talking to my working husband, I asked him to take me out for dinner. He couldn't be due to work, requesting that I cook instead. I cooked half-heartedly, realizing it wasn't good. When my husband arrived, he thanked me with a smile after eating, despite the meal's quality.

I didn't understand his gratitude until later. His "thank you" showed he appreciated my effort, even if I didn't cook well. I was taken aback by his understanding. His thank-you changed my perspective. Now, even when making tea, I do it with love and care, not for appreciation but to bring joy to those I serve.

How often do we thank those who cook for us? Regardless of taste, cooking requires effort, patience, and love. Take time to appreciate it. Even a simple thank-you adds flavor to life.

23. The Night Intruder

Marriage imparts numerous lessons. Some are bitter, while others are sweet. A person's married life is ongoing, much like the process of preparing Biryani. Many spices are involved, requiring hours of tedious preparation, resulting in a delicious feast.

I haven't been married long enough to offer advice, but there have been incidents that changed and molded me, making me both cry and laugh. One such incident that I often reminisce about and laugh about involves encountering a cockroach. Yes, you heard it right—a COCKROACH!

My typical day starts with waking up (I'm always a bit late), hurriedly preparing breakfast, packing lunches for my husband and myself, and rushing to work. After work, I head to the gym, return, finish household chores, and finally settle down for some writing when my husband returns from work. That's our time to chat, have dinner, and then go to bed.

One day, as usual, after completing all the chores, I was tired from a long day at work. I eagerly waited for my husband to return so we could chat and unwind. Finally, when he arrived, he settled with his tablet to watch a comedy show. While he laughed and enjoyed the show, I grew increasingly annoyed. Every time I tried to get his attention, he ignored me. To make matters worse, he suggested I join him in watching the program, which irritated me more than entertained me.

I waited for him to put down the tablet, but he didn't. We had dinner, went to bed, and the tablet was still with him. Losing patience, I eventually screamed and started a fight. We argued, I cried, and after a dramatic exchange, we slept facing away from each other. We'd had our disagreements like any couple, but until that day, we had never gone to bed angry. Deep down, I knew we wouldn't resolve things that day; my husband was angrier than usual. Although I felt guilty, my ego prevented me from apologizing. Sleep eluded me. I tossed and turned and cried out loud, but nothing seemed to help.

Feeling helpless, I eventually got up and turned on the light. To my shock, there was a massive cockroach on the bed. I leaped out, screaming and attempting to wake my husband. My scream startled the cockroach, causing it to scurry into my husband's T-shirt. It moved around inside, making me laugh and driving my husband into a frenzy. After a lot of commotion, we managed to capture and remove the cockroach. Both of us burst into laughter! While ensuring there were no more intruders, we went back to sleep, this time facing each other. That's when we realized we had been fighting.

By then, it was too late to bring up the argument; we had already reconciled! Silently, I thanked the giant cockroach in my heart. Neither of us wanted to sleep angry, but we didn't know how to fix it. Though the cockroach was a troublesome and unwelcome guest, this tiny creature brought us back together. Even today, the sight of a cockroach terrifies me, but it never fails to remind me of the incident that helped us reconcile.

24. What About Your "Me" Time?

Writing has always been my passion. Penning down my thoughts was, is, and has been the best part of my life, until I got married.

Most of you might have heard of the famous comedian Russell Peters; he eloquently explains how the brains of men and women work. It might seem funny, but there is absolute truth in his talk. He says women can think about hundreds of things at a time, whereas men can focus on only one thing at a time.

This is what happened to me after I got married—my mind deviated, I did a lot of things, and my hobbies and preferences slowly started taking a backseat. The world around me conveniently pacified me, saying it was an adjustment and completely normal. Managing the house, working, cooking, and taking care of the family was beautiful, but amidst all this, I was missing something. I was missing "me."

As a working woman, I felt balancing work and home was my all-time biggest achievement, and I didn't think I needed to do anything more. Slowly, this attitude turned into laziness, and eventually, the spare time I had turned into time spent in front of the TV or on my mobile, while everything else took a backseat.

On a typical day, as I was sitting with my husband watching television, he started praising the actress whose movie we were watching, saying she was a complete woman. He went on to compliment her talents and how skillfully she managed her career.

As usual, my instincts made me jealous, and I started to argue, saying it was easier for her with all the help she had, whereas I had no extra hands and yet managed the home and work as a career woman. Listening to this, my husband quietly told me that I was indeed a complete woman. He went on to say that balancing work and home wasn't easy, and he was proud of me. However, he asked me if I was truly happy. If I was, he had no issues, but if not, it was time for me to reflect and start doing what truly made me happy.

I pondered for a while and realized a harsh truth: that actress was bold enough to live her dreams and showcase her talents to the world. But what was I doing with the talents God had blessed me with? Along with being a perfect employee, wife, daughter-in-law, and daughter, was I truly doing what I loved?

That's when I decided that every day, I would reserve "me" time, but this time wouldn't be just for movies or chatting—it would be for my writing. Every day, for a little while, I decided to set aside my work and household responsibilities and do what made me happy. That's when I decided to take my writing seriously. I realized that to be called special, we need to infuse a bit of the extraordinary into our ordinary lives. To stand out, we must tap into our uniqueness and nurture it. This would not only make us happy and fulfilled, but also make those around us proud. So, I began to write again and never looked back.

I've heard many of my friends say, "I used to sing before," "I used to act in plays," "I was interested in Origami," etc. Well, remove "used to" and decide to do it now. It's all in our minds. Don't carry regrets in life—do all that you wish to. Sing if you wish to, dance, hit the gym, bake a cake, stitch a dress—do anything and everything that brings you joy and helps develop the talents within you.

Maybe the entire world won't recognize you, but make sure that at least a few acknowledge the talent within you. Don't let it fade away.

Each of us is gifted. Our talents might not be the same, but our abilities are. It's never too late to start doing what you've always wanted and to make yourself happy.

Remember, in the end, you are complete when you are "you."

25. VAT 69

The initial days of marriage are difficult to forget. They are made up of bittersweet experiences that one carries throughout their lifetime. It was no different in my life. Since ours was an arranged marriage, our conversations and intimacy during the courtship period were limited. We hardly met once a fortnight for a couple of hours. After marriage, when we started living together, the unspoken urge to be with each other, the stolen kisses, and the night walks were the most sought-after. However, the messy cupboards, laundry, and chores came along with them.

My husband and I have been married for ten years. During these years, we have faced innumerable experiences as a couple. There have been funny and hilarious incidents, along with ugly and sad ones. Some days, we do not even want to reminisce, while others we long to relive. One such funny incident that my husband still recalls and laughs his heart out about is that of VAT 69!

Surprised? Read along.

We did not have a long honeymoon. Due to family constraints, we restricted our outing to a two-day stay in a hill station. We had longed to travel together. After two months of marriage, we booked a stay in Coorg. We were all geared up and looking forward to it. We had to travel to Mangalore for a family function, after which we directly drove to Coorg. I was still a new bride and was getting accustomed to the new phase of life. I was always cautious and tried to remain meek and humble. As I was an only child, I was brought up with lots of love, respect, and freedom. Along with it, my parents made sure I was disciplined and inculcated strong family values in me. During my courtship period, I remember my parents telling me to respect my elders and be tolerant. An important lesson my dad taught me was never to splurge money unnecessarily. He guided me and instructed me to plan my finances and use the funds systematically. True to his words, from the first few days of marriage, I did not initiate any unnecessary spending and stopped my husband from spending anything that we felt was not necessary.

For our trip, we set a budget and chose a place to accommodate it. We had decided not to exceed the budget and to spend reasonably. One major point I had insisted on was not buying anything at the resort. From prior experiences, it was clear that the prices in resorts were very high, so we decided to go out for our meals instead of having them in the resort. The day we arrived, it was late afternoon and raining heavily. My husband told me he was too tired to drive again for lunch and that it was okay to order just one meal from the resort kitchen. Though I was a little reluctant, I did not want to trouble my husband and agreed, then called room service for the menu.

Once the menu arrived, my husband glanced through it and handed it over to me before going for a shower, leaving me responsible for ordering. Even to this day, my husband does not prefer ordering, and the responsibility is always thrust upon me. Though he complains about my choices at times, he still feels I am pickier and that it would be better for me to order, and he would adjust to my choices.

I began to glance through the menu, and as I had suspected, the prices were exorbitant. Left with no choice, I opted for two dishes—a simple curry and rice—and closed the menu. Just then, my husband screamed from inside, asking me to order a drink. He said he preferred either a good cocktail or a glass of chilled beer. I reopened the menu and began searching for beverages, and just then, I came across the page with an array of cocktails. I was taken aback by the prices. Every cocktail was priced above Rs. 300. Still confused about what to order, I turned the page and saw a wide selection of whiskey and Scotch. Finally, after thinking for a while, I decided on a drink and called for room service. My eyes fell to the bottom of the page, where it mentioned VAT 69. Being a commerce postgraduate, I knew about VAT but not about VAT 69. Still, I assumed it to be some kind of tax on the drinks since it was at the bottom of the page. The amount mentioned was Rs. 400. When I looked at the cocktail I had planned to order, it cost Rs. 375. I thought it would be pointless to pay Rs. 400 as tax for a cocktail of Rs. 375. So I dropped the idea of ordering it. I knew I could convince my husband to drink water and called room service, placing the order only for food and waiting for my husband to come out.

After a few minutes, the food arrived. We were very hungry, so we gobbled up the food in silence. After finishing half the meal, my husband asked me if I had ordered something to drink. I replied in the negative, and he was crestfallen. He asked me why I hadn't ordered a drink, and I had my answer ready. I explained to him how expensive the drinks were and also reminded him of our decision not to exceed the budget. He further inquired about the cost. When I told him the price of the cocktail and the VAT of Rs. 400, he was shocked and not entirely convinced. Sulking a little, he finished his meal. After the room service came in and cleared the table, we retired to bed and started discussing our next plan.

Just then, my husband asked me to pass the menu card, which was on my side of the bed. I was a little hesitant to give it to him, fearing he would order a cocktail. He assured me that he would just look at the prices and not order anything. While he was skimming through the menu with confidence, I turned the page and showed him the VAT 69 charge of Rs. 400, justifying why I hadn't ordered a drink for him. Looking at it, my husband faintly laughed and asked me if I knew what that was. I told him I knew it was a tax charged on drinks. Listening to this, my husband burst out laughing. He rolled on the bed and continued to laugh. I didn't realize what was happening, and what I had done that had made him laugh uncontrollably. Pulling himself together, he told me that VAT 69 was not a tax but the name of an Indian Whiskey. Hearing this, I was embarrassed beyond explanation. I was embarrassed that being a commerce graduate, I did not have clarity about taxes, and I was even more embarrassed by my assumption that Whiskey was being taxed.

I kept quiet, walked out, and sat alone. My husband came to me and consoled me, saying it was okay. He said it was sheer innocence and not stupidity. Though I wasn't fully convinced and still embarrassed beyond words, my husband ordered two cocktails, and we both drank them in utter silence, looking blankly at each other.

This fiasco did not end here. Even to this day, my husband makes it a point to narrate the incident to every new person he meets. He still laughs his heart out, and I am still embarrassed, just like the day it happened. Every time we look at the menu, he reminds me that it is a drink and not a tax!

26. Story After Marriage: With a Drizzle of Coconut Oil and Pepper

To start, I wish to dedicate this write-up to my dear husband – the one who reads only those articles in which he's mentioned. As for the rest, he either chooses to ignore them or makes me read them aloud so he can continue with his other "important" pursuits. Well, that pretty much sums up my life after marriage.

I thought this could be my best opportunity to write about this topic. I don't often venture into writing love stories, or anything even mildly related to romance.

Recently, as part of a campaign, my husband and I shot a video of baking a cake and uploaded photos of the cake with wine on the side and the beautiful ambiance we had set up at home. We received numerous compliments, and most of them were about how romantic it all looked. Well, the setup was indeed romantic, but the clutter and dishes to wash after the episode were even more romantic! On a serious note, many married couples often complain that at the beginning of the marriage or during the courtship period, their spouse was so romantic, but as the years pass, the romance fizzles out and married life turns stale, devoid of any spark.

I too have complained a lot and personally wondered, where have all the spark and butterflies in the stomach gone? Slowly, I realized they have completely disappeared—just like my slim figure and my husband's four (six according to him!) packs.

Life after marriage is certainly different. To put it better, it has evolved. Long romantic messages slowly turn into grocery lists. Tight jeans and cocktail dresses are replaced by pajamas. Shea butter cream is replaced by Vick's gel. Soft kisses become formal pecks. Yet, we claim that we are in love. Or are we?

I remember an incident during our courtship period when I had slipped and sprained my leg. My fiancé (now husband) rushed to my aid, helped me sit, massaged my leg, applied ice, and enquired about my well-being multiple times. Recently, history repeated itself—I slipped again and landed on the floor in our room. To my utter dismay, my husband was busy looking at the floor instead of me. When I enquired about what he was doing, he calmly replied that he was checking if the marbles on the floor were intact and hadn't broken because of my fall! Well, priorities change! However, afterward, he did lift me and applied a good amount of pain-relieving gel. Nevertheless, there was a huge difference in his reaction. This did make me realize that life after marriage had a lot of chilies but less spice!

Life was different before marriage or even a few months after marriage. We would look into each other's eyes and smile all day. But now, we are better off looking at our smartphones than looking at each other. Before marriage, we would speak over the phone for hours, and now calls are meant only for important conversations. Before marriage, we longed for privacy, just to steal a warm hug. But now, we prefer some "me" time over "us" time. In the early days of marriage, a kiss was mandatory before going to work, and now kisses are restricted to Christmas and Easter wishes. Yet, we proudly claim we are so much in love. Or are we?

While I was planning to write this piece, a series of questions crossed my mind. How would people accept this? Would they be offended? Am I propagating negative aspects of marriage? But the most crucial question I asked myself was, are we still in love? After pondering for quite some time, I realized that probably "love" is cliché and overrated. What I understood was that we were committed and attached to each other. That's what glued us together when we felt we had fallen out of love.

There are moments in each couple's life when they feel there is no love between them. But is it true? For most of us in the present generation, the definition of love is vastly different. It's about romance, vacation, cuddling, intimacy, and freedom. Probably we're forgetting the aspects of companionship, trust, transparency, security, and dependency. Aren't we?

I've heard many married couples say, "I don't want to be dependent on anyone; I am independent." Well, being independent is appreciated, but a beautiful marriage involves some level of dependency that adds a different flavor to love. I'm dependent on my husband in many ways. I rely on him when picking a dress or making important decisions like switching jobs or pursuing an interest. I depend on him when selecting a piece of furniture and many other things. These dependencies of the couple bind us to each other. Seeking each other's opinions fosters transparency and builds trust and compatibility.

I've heard people say, "I want freedom!" I've said this many times too. But what is freedom? When a concerned wife frantically calls her husband to check on his safety, is it curtailing her freedom? When a husband who struggles with finances advises his spouse to spend less, is it curtailing his freedom? Even today, when I wish to buy something, I discuss it with my husband, and he does the same when planning expenses. Even when making plans to go out or meet friends, we inform each other and seek each other's opinions. It's not about control; it's about involvement.

People grow and change, and so does a married couple. As the years pass, we mature, and so do our thoughts. While love remains intact, it's expressed differently. Today, when I leave for work, my husband doesn't kiss me and say, "I miss you." But he helps me during busy mornings and waves a gentle goodbye. Most of our outings today aren't long drives, but short stopovers for a glass of wine and peaceful moments. It's not about passionate sex, but long hugs and the reassurance that someone is sleeping by your side.

I've received tremendous support from my husband. When I planned to switch careers, taking a huge risk, he wholeheartedly supported me, even though we weren't financially secure. Whenever I wanted to dedicate time to pursue my interests, he never stopped me or questioned why. Those evenings when I didn't want to cook, he quietly had a bowl of Maggi or some leftover rice. Those times when I didn't look pretty and my voice cracked, he smiled and held my hand. What could be more romantic than this? This was more than romance. This was commitment. This was fulfilling the promise we made before God to stand by each other not only in times of fun and frolic but also in tears and fights.

The greatest test of our marriage was the loss of our babies. When I went through two miscarriages, I witnessed what love was. My husband not only held me close and tight but also helped me step out of the pain at every turn. His love and care wouldn't allow him to pressure me for a child to this day. Isn't this more beautiful than red roses and a bottle of wine?

Each of us has our own struggles in marriage. There are times we scream at each other and wonder why we got into this. We hate to look at each other and wish time would fly. We want to run far away and hide. But when it's all over, isn't it our spouse that we want by our side?

Ten years of married life aren't long, but they're not short either. We face new challenges every day. There are arguments, fights, doubts, and tears. But they're nothing compared to the fact that God has given us the most precious gift. A friend sent specially for each of us. Yes, it won't always be the same. There may not be surprises of expensive gifts. There may not always be a romantic getaway, and each other's habits may pull us apart. But the love will always stay. It has stayed for me too. When he helps me in the kitchen, when he arranges the vessels, when he respects my folks when he discusses his problems and weaknesses, when he lays open his vulnerabilities and issues, when he fights with me to watch Netflix, when he applauds my success when he cracks a joke, when he can't stand to see my tears, when he argues, when he lies to make me happy when he works hard to secure my future, when he calls me when I'm far away—these moments remind me every day that this is love.

Though marriage has many aspects, the fact that we're glued together emits an aroma just like coconut oil. No matter what ingredients you put in a dish, coconut oil outshines them all, just like the love between a couple. As years pass by, the spark might disappear, but the shine remains. Yes, we'll continue to sigh and wonder why. There will be fights and arguments, just like pepper. But though pepper is spice, it's digested well by our bodies. Every after-marriage story isn't sparkly white, but it's tempered with a drizzle of coconut oil and some spice.

27. An Honest Reply from a Husband

I once went to a party with my wife. Convincing her was a struggle; she declined a couple of times, citing sickness and tiredness. Finally, she admitted that she didn't have the right kind of clothes to wear. After convincing her and assuring her that she would look good in whatever she wore, she agreed.

That evening, she chose a long, black gown—she always wore black. I knew why.

She brushed her short hair and clipped it from behind. She applied a thin layer of cream and some lipstick and looked in the mirror, but she did so without smiling. She walked beside me and sat quietly.

The party was an extravagant affair; the room was filled with a vivacious and joyful crowd, all swaying to the beats of the music. After exchanging initial greetings, I found my friends and left my wife behind, running to join them. She sat in a corner with a little wine in hand. After a couple of minutes, I glanced around to see her; she was busy chatting with a lady, and I was happy she had found company.

I continued the conversation with my friends, and just then my best friend made a rather sad remark. He looked at me, glanced over at my wife, and said, "What a pair." I knew he was being sarcastic, but I chose to ignore him. He continued and asked me how I could live with her. He told me, "You are tall, fair, and handsome. Look at her; she is chubby, fat, and hardly pretty." He told me I still had time and that I could rethink my decision and choose someone pretty and fine.

I knew I could ignore him, but this time I had to speak up and bare my heart. I gently replied to him, "Yes, sometimes I wish she were tender and slim. Sometimes my mind wanders away when I look at a pretty woman passing by, but I have tried a million times to convince my heart. It always chooses my wife again and again."

Every morning, when I wake up to the smell of brewing coffee and an aromatic breakfast, I don't look at my wife's figure or face. Instead, I admire her patience and care.

Every morning, as she struggles and juggles to cook lunch for me, packs my tiffin, and rushes to work, I don't admire the size of her waist. Instead, I stand in awe of her dedication and her utmost grace.

Every evening, when I come home and see the welcoming smile on her face, I forget all my pains and remember that I have someone. No matter what I do, those efforts will never go in vain.

Every evening, when I enjoy the sumptuous dinner prepared by her, I don't usually stare at her bust. Instead, I marvel at the genuine effort she puts in every time she cooks a meal.

When I crash on the sofa and look around to find a neat and clean home, I don't think about her slender legs. Instead, I thank her for her hardworking nature and her trait of cleanliness.

When I am sick and tired, she wakes up every hour to check on me and comfort me. Then I am not looking for a well-dressed model; I am looking for her tender arms to wrap around me and give me warmth.

When I'm at work and feeling dejected because my efforts seem fruitless, I'm not looking for a night of intimacy. I'm relieved and uplifted when she listens to me patiently, comforts me, and assures me that my efforts will never go to waste.

When I wanted to pursue my hobbies and no one encouraged me, when I felt lost in the crowd, my eyes didn't search for a girl with a perfect jawline. Instead, I looked for her tender face. Her motivation and push made me climb the ladder and try again, even though I failed in the past.

When she treats my family like her own and goes out of her way to help others in need, I don't worry about her curves. Instead, I thank those who raised her, teaching her the morals of love and care.

When she pursues her hobbies relentlessly and makes a name for herself, I don't sit and admire her well-shaped fingernails or well-kept hair. Instead, I stand and clap for her determination and amazing talent.

When she cracks her jokes and makes me laugh, when she passes her hand through my hair and caresses me, when she sings loudly and cheers me up, even when she sighs at my slightest frown, that's when I know she is the one.

At the end of the day, when we kneel to pray, when we hold hands and dedicate our lives to the one above, that's when I remember our vows every day.

I continued to tell him, "The women you ridicule, saying they're fat, were not always so. Circumstances and situations have made them that way. She's trying her best. However, she is, and she's the best. Her body may or may not change, but what will not change is her heart. Her perfect smile, her innocent look, her tantalizing personality"

She is my wife, the one I adore. She is the woman, the mother of my children. She is mine—forever, only mine. Saying this, I looked at him and smiled. I got up and walked toward my lovely wife. I held her close, planted a soft kiss on her cheek, and strode away proudly. This time she walked beside me with a few tears in her eyes and a bright smile.

28. An Unspoken Pledge

I, (name), take you, (name), to be my spouse. I promise to stand by you in good times and bad, in sickness and health. I will love and honor you all my life.

This vow is exchanged by couples at Christian weddings. They're expected to follow and fulfill this pledge throughout their marriage. While thinking about this vow, I thought it would be good to add another line: "I will support you, stand by you, and defend you, even when others are angry with you."

You heard me right. You might be wondering why. The answer is simple. Today, couples are supposed to care for each other when one is ill, provide financial support, share household duties, and raise children together—everything is about sharing. Applause for the progressive mindset! But sadly, there's one aspect where it's expected that a husband shouldn't support his wife when his family is upset with her.

Recently, my friend told me about her colleague's sad situation when we met for coffee. Her colleague, a talented young woman in her late twenties, had been married for four years. Right from the start, she faced restrictions and conditions at her in-laws' home. She couldn't pursue her passions, work shifts, or even get help with chores. Despite this, she managed to have a happy life. But things changed when an accident left her with mobility issues in her hand. Her husband hired a helper to assist her, which upset her in-laws. Supporting his wife caused problems, leading to their marriage falling apart. Hearing this saddened me and made me think about the fragility of relationships today.

People often say, "A daughter is a daughter forever, but a son is a son until he's married." How wrong is that? Whenever I hear this, it's demeaning and disappointing. Daughters and sons love their parents equally, but parents expect a daughter to be welcomed and cared for by her husband and in-laws. Yet they forget that a son who's married is responsible too. In families with both sons and daughters, parents expect the daughter to be respected at her in-laws' home. If anything goes wrong, they hold the son-in-law accountable. They want him to stand by their daughter, but when a similar situation happens in their family and their son supports the daughter-in-law, it's seen as a crime. Isn't that hypocrisy?

In TV shows and movies today, family issues often involve the daughter-in-law or mother-in-law. While clichéd, these portrayals reflect real-life problems stemming from ego and gossip. When parents-in-law have issues with the daughter-in-law, they discuss it with everyone except her. Similar things happen when the daughter-in-law faces problems. I wonder why. If they both tried sitting down to discuss their issues, I believe they'd find solutions. Gossiping about family members with outsiders only creates division and sadness. Spreading gossip like wildfire only brings embarrassment to the family.

Another negative trait we see today is blowing up small mistakes made by daughters-in-law or parents-in-law. In families where both a daughter and a daughter-in-law live, the daughter's mistakes are downplayed while the daughter-in-law's are exaggerated, causing unnecessary chaos. The daughter-in-law forgives her parents' mistakes more easily than her in-laws'. It's important for everyone to remember that humans make mistakes, and exaggerating them isn't helpful.

Mistakes should be addressed gently to allow correction without making a fuss.

Divorce rates have risen nowadays. While couples are often the main reason, family interference and constant nagging also play a role in separation. Many brides struggle to adapt to their husband's family customs. When couples decide to move out and start their own family, the bride is often blamed as a homewrecker. What's the better choice? Living separately with love, or staying together and fighting daily until things explode? Also, why is living separately always seen as the wife's decision? Maybe the husband suggested it. I'm not suggesting leaving your parents and living apart. But if parents are independent and the couple believes that living separately could improve their relationship, why not? It's ironic that when a son gets an opportunity to work abroad, parents are proud, but if he wants to live nearby, it's considered wrong. There's no logic in that, right?

In all of this, it's usually the son or husband who's caught in the middle. Men often face stress trying to keep peace in the family. If a husband stands by his wife and supports her, parents might not take it well. The daughter-in-law is often blamed too. People might say her parents brainwashed him. That's absurd and baseless. Is the man so clueless that he can't tell right from wrong? It's crucial for a husband to support his wife. Not when she's wrong, but when she's right and fighting for her basic needs. Supporting her doesn't mean disrespecting her parents. He vowed to support his wife during marriage. To keep that promise, he should stand by her no matter what. In family conflicts, the focus is usually on the daughter-in-law, but it's the husband or son who bears the brunt. It's sad to see him struggling to keep them both happy, yet getting no credit. Instead, they're emotionally tormented from all sides.

For any woman, an identity crisis is a major setback. After marriage, some parents distance themselves from their daughter, making her believe her husband's house is her only world. But if she chooses to live with her in-laws, she'll never be seen as a family member. Her likes and dislikes are restricted. She can't touch cupboards or change interiors as she pleases. Where does she belong? If a son's wife is welcomed as a daughter-in-law, she should be treated equally and allowed to contribute. She's often seen as an outsider, though. She can't even ask her husband for help with chores without being seen as dominating. If she's sick, she can't rest. She's called lazy, her cooking is criticized, and her talents aren't appreciated. Why? If she's called a daughter-in-law, why isn't she treated like one?

Family fights often escalate due to interference from others. When family disagreements involve outsiders, things get worse. In some families, issues with the daughter-in-law are discussed with extended family members, who judge without knowing the full story. The daughter-in-law might be treated as an outcast and needlessly taunted. On the other hand, she shares details of fights with her family and friends, who advise without understanding, causing more harm. Families should realize it's better to talk to each other than about each other. Seeking help from a neutral family counselor or religious figure could also be beneficial.

Please don't think I'm irrational in favoring daughters-in-law or that this article is biased towards them. I am a daughter-in-law, and my friends are also married women my age, so I see these issues from their viewpoint. Family conflicts involving daughters-in-law are often treated lightly, even in the media. But I want to highlight the mental strain it causes. Both parties experience significant stress that often goes unnoticed. Yet sympathy is often reserved for parents, while daughters-in-law are blamed.

When a son supports his wife and doesn't side with his parents during disagreements, he's criticized. He's seen as having changed and become his wife's follower. Outsiders and family members warn of parental curses. Nowadays, using teachings from priests as hints is a new trend, especially in my community. God's word is forwarded to provoke and insult. Do we understand these curses? Doesn't God see the tears of daughters-in-law and sons? Threatening in the name of God or using His words to defame others is wrong. Instead, these powerful words can bring positive change.

This article doesn't judge or point fingers. It aims to make society aware of reality. Advertisements and movies talk about sending parents to care homes and dowry harassment. But they often ignore the consequences of daily family squabbles. These might seem minor, but many women aren't empowered enough to handle them. Small issues can snowball into major problems, especially when husbands turn against their wives. This has led to divorces and even suicides. It's time for society and close circles to support both parties and help them find resolutions. Husbands should stand by their wives, no matter the situation. Point out mistakes, but don't abandon each other—both husband and wife are responsible for each other's well-being until the end.

The family is a beautiful institution. Let's not allow ego, anger, gossip, lies, or possessiveness to ruin it. Embrace differences and live happily together.

29. "The Naughty One"

Growing up without a pet, I never truly understood what it meant to have one. My interactions with dogs and cats were only during my visits to my native home during the summer vacation. Most of the time, I preferred to observe them from a distance when they were tied up, and I would hide and watch them when they were set free. I always wondered how people could love pets so much. It felt funny to me when I saw people cry and wail when something happened to their pets. I felt weird and failed to understand their emotions. Throughout my childhood, I never preferred the company of a pet and never dared to hold any little animal in my hand.

After I got married, I was fortunate to become a part of a family that was deeply into dogs, especially my mother-in-law. The house I married into had a dog named Tarzan, who had been a part of the family for many years. Initially, when I first arrived, I felt scared, but eventually, I befriended him, and he started enjoying my company. I, too, started forming a bond with him. However, somewhere deep down, I still didn't develop a strong attachment and wondered what it would be like to truly be attached to a pet.

One Sunday afternoon, my mother-in-law suddenly appeared with this small, cute pup. When I looked at it for the first time, something in my heart stirred. The first time I held it in my arms was probably the best moment. Its small, tiny, inviting eyes just captivated me. I was filled with mixed emotions, not knowing what to do with this little one. After a lot of arguments and discussions, we decided to keep this small wonder in our home for a few days. We reached a consensus that we would keep it for a short while so that my little niece could play with it, and later, we would put it up for adoption.

The days that followed were like a roller coaster ride for us. His barking, playfulness, feeding him, and taking care of him became our daily routine. I had always dreamed of naming my pup Babloo, and so we named this tiny wonder Babloo. Babloo had officially become the smallest member of our small family. All of us enjoyed his company, and somehow he had secured a permanent position in our family. I had particularly become very close to him, and since I was staying at home, my continuous conversations were with him. He had become my friend and a source of comfort in my moments of loneliness.

Then, one fine evening, our little Baloo disappeared. I don't know how he vanished, and his absence was the worst phase. We searched for him frantically in the streets and in everyone's houses, but no one seemed to have seen him. Every time I thought of him, I whispered a small prayer and asked God to bring him back to me. Three days had passed, and no one knew what had happened to this little, naughty pup of ours. There was a gloominess in the house; my mother-in-law was devastated, and I couldn't control my tears. During all this, I realized that, knowingly or unknowingly, I had formed an attachment with the dog—an attachment that I had never understood when he was near. I had never thought I would cry for an animal, but this little, tiny pup had left an indelible mark on my heart.

During my grief, I began to understand the deep attachment that pet owners have for their pets. I truly grasped how someone could love animals unconditionally. I began to understand what it means to love a pet. This small, four-legged little fellow, without even uttering a word, had instilled in me selfless love and etched a permanent place in my heart.

Then, to our astonishment, after three days, our little Babloo arrived at our doorstep, standing there majestically and happily. Our joy knew no bounds, and all of us leaped in joy. I felt relieved and extremely happy to see him back, but to this day, all of us are in a dilemma as to what had happened to him during those three days, where he had disappeared, and who had brought him back. Somewhere deep in my heart, I know it was the Almighty who had planned this. He had taken Babloo away so that I would realize the value of that little one. He was also mighty enough to give him back to us and fill our family with happiness once again.

Eventually, when I had to return to work, we had to give away Babloo. Another loving family adopted him, and he is living a beautiful life. It's been five years since we gave him away, but every time I see a dog, I remember our little Babloo. I keep wondering how it would be to have him close and nearby. One thing I am sure of is that no matter how many dogs we adopt or other pets we bring home, our little Babloo will always remain my first love.

www.ingramcontent.com/pod-product-compliance
Lightning Source LLC
LaVergne TN
LVHW091120150826
845673LV00002B/913

* 9 7 9 8 8 9 1 3 3 9 3 5 4 *